"This is not just a book by the distinguished educator Dr. William Mitchell—it's down-to-earth Billy Mitchell writing zestfully about how all of us can shed the weights that keep us from being everything we should be. There's a hands-on approach to successful living in these pages, yet this wise and entertaining author never lets us forget how important it is to factor God into our day-to-day."

Van Varner, Editorial Director
GUIDEPOSTS

"When Dr. Norman Vincent Peale introduced us in 1987, he referred to Bill Mitchell as a 'kindred spirit.' Reading *Winning in the Land of Giants* more than proves the point. In his practical ideas, drawn from biblical wisdom and proven through the lives of everyday people, Bill has once again revealed the truth that all of us have a great destiny, an ability to overcome our small thinking to win great victories."

Eric J. Fellman, President and CEO
Peale Center for Christian Living

"Chaos seems to be the nature of our current society, which makes reading *Winning in the Land of Giants* an important assignment. It will help you get in touch with your divine nature and immediately put you on track to focusing on the meaningful priorities in life."

Roger Staubach, Chairman and CEO
The Staubach Company
NFL Hall of Fame

"This book is marvelous and inspiring. America's institutions and spirit would be renewed and invigorated if Americans would read and receive the stirring message of this winning book. Dr. William Mitchell is the able torchbearer for the late Dr. Norman Vincent Peale."

Dr. Byrle Kynerd, Superintendent
Briarwood Christian School
Birmingham, Alabama

"Since the loss to our world of Dr. Norman Vincent Peale, Bill Mitchell, in my opinion, has emerged as the world's most positive person. *Winning in the Land of Giants,* the latest testament by the author of *The Power of Positive Students,* can be used as a beacon or lighthouse by persons in all walks of life to help them heal those temporary feelings of doubt, low-esteem, inadequacy, lack of self-worth or self-confidence. This book is a must for the personal libraries of all potential 'giant slayers.'"

Dr. Harold C. Carl II, Superintendent
Pleasants County Schools
St. Mary's, West Virginia

"Dr. William Mitchell's new book, *Winning in the Land of Giants,* is *must* reading for every administrator, teacher, and parent in America. Dr. Mitchell has provided the clearest picture I have seen of some of the fundamental principles to prepare us for life's challenges.

Anyone who reads this book will be compelled to use the content with family and friends."

Dr. Jack Cockrill, Superintendent
McKinney Independent School District
McKinney, Texas

"Dr. Mitchell accurately explains how our attitudes affect our perceptions of ourselves and others. Parents and teachers need to read this book to help understand and support our most valuable asset, our children."

Frederick N. Brown, President
National Association of Elementary School
Principals

"Dr. Bill Mitchell has done it again. With deep insight he challenges us to become all that we can be. The principles are practical. The impact will be life-changing. Get ready to soar."

Dr. John Tolson, Founder and Chairman
The Gathering of Men—USA, Inc.
Founder, NBA Chapel Program

"The only things that are going to take you from where you are now to where you are going to be five years from now are the books you read and the people you meet. I can't control the people you are going to meet, but I can tell you that *Winning in the Land of Giants* is a very, very positive book, and I have to believe it will have a positive influence on your performance and your attitude."

Lou Holtz, Head Coach
University of Notre Dame Football

"As the title fittingly implies, this book has *enormous* impact and *great* importance and will make a *huge,* positive difference in all it touches. Dr. William Mitchell lives his words, turning parents into leaders, children into champions, and employees into entrepreneurs. His teachings make the smallest feel the tallest!"

Dr. Denis Waitley, Author
Empires of the Mind

"Bill Mitchell is one of the great positive thinkers in our country. His book *Winning in the Land of Giants* is a must-read for all those who have ever doubted themselves. You, too, can become a giant slayer!"

Ken Blanchard, Coauthor
The One Minute Manager

"Leadership is about creating an environment whereby individuals of all ages, races, religions, and cultural backgrounds can realize their potential. Bill Mitchell's book *Winning in the Land of Giants* provides powerful examples of effective leaders successfully applying the basic building blocks—hard work, spiritual values, self-determination, and positive attitudes—to better their organizations and the people in them."

Les Alberthal, Chairman, President, and CEO
Electronic Data Systems

WINNING
IN THE
LAND
OF
GIANTS

Dr. William Mitchell

THOMAS NELSON PUBLISHERS
Nashville • Atlanta • London • Vancouver

Published in Nashville, Tennessee, by Thomas Nelson, Inc., Publishers, and distributed in Canada by Word Communications, Ltd., Richmond, British Columbia.

Every effort has been made to contact the owners or owners' agents of copyrighted material for permission to use their material. If copyrighted material has been included without the correct copyright notice or without permission, due to error or failure to locate owners/agents or otherwise, we apologize for the error or omission and ask that the owner or owner's agent contact Oliver-Nelson and supply appropriate information. Correct information will be included in any reprinting.

Unless otherwise noted, the Bible version used in this publication is THE NEW KING JAMES VERSION. Copyright © 1979, 1980, 1982, 1990, Thomas Nelson, Inc., Publishers.

Verses marked TLB are taken from *The Living Bible,* copyright 1971 by Tyndale House Publishers, Wheaton, IL. Used by permission.

The story on Alabama football coach Gene Stallings in chapter 5 is based on a January 3, 1993, newspaper article written by Clyde Bolton, the sports columnist for *The Birmingham News.*

Library of Congress Cataloging-in-Publication Data

Mitchell, William, 1932–
    Winning in the land of giants / William Mitchell.
        p.   cm.
    ISBN 0-7852-8094-4 (alk. paper)
        1. Self-confidence—Religious aspects—Christianity. 2. Self-esteem—Religious aspects—Christianity. 3. Success—Religious aspects—Christianity. I. Title.
    BV4598.23.M57 1995
    248.4—dc20   95–13410
                                                                         CIP

Printed in the United States of America.
1 2 3 4 5 6 — 00 99 98 97 96 95

TO

This book is dedicated to my
family: Carolyn, my wife of 42
years—together we have slain
many giants; my sons, Billy
and Mike; my daughter-in-law,
Janey; and my two beautiful
grandchildren, Michelle and
Matthew, a new generation of
winners in the land of giants!

God had special people in
mind when He made
this family.

CONTENTS

ACKNOWLEDGMENTS

I want to say a special thank-you to the following men:

Dr. Wayne Brown, my pastor at First Baptist Church in Myrtle Beach, South Carolina. He gives 110 percent to God every day and is a great role model for every church member, teaching by example the importance and power of prayer.

Rev. Harold Lewis, pastor of Belin United Methodist Church in Murrells Inlet, South Carolina, where my son Mike, his wife, Janey, and their two children, Michelle and Matthew, are members. He can preach the best twenty-five-minute sermon I have ever heard. People can't wait to return to his church.

Dr. Dick Lincoln, pastor of the Shandon Baptist Church in Columbia, South Carolina, where my son Billy is a member. Each week I receive an audiotape of his powerful, biblical messages. On any Sunday, he will make all of us who listen to his message squirm a little.

Dr. Bill Bouknight, formerly pastor of the First United Methodist Church in Myrtle Beach and currently pastor of Christ United Methodist Church in Memphis, Tennessee. I enjoyed watching Reverend Bouknight on television because he always preached a challenging, inspiring message. One of his messages, "Don't Forget the Basics," gave me the idea to write the chapter on "Sticking with the Basics."

Each of these exceptionally talented men of God has preached messages that have recently "filled my cup" and inspired me to write this book.

Additionally, I would like to thank the following for their television ministries that have, over the years, been most helpful to me as I strive to become a giant slayer: Drs. Billy Graham, Pat Robertson, Robert Schuller, D. James Kennedy, Charles Stanley, and Jerry Falwell.

I want to express gratitude to the late Dr. Norman Vincent Peale, who taught us many important lessons, including the importance of "keeping our cups filled." He, no doubt, is filling cups today in heaven.

These preachers, like all of us, are not flawless, but they have touched millions of lives, including mine.

Also, I would like to acknowledge the entire Thomas Nelson Publishers team. Having been a coach, principal, and superintendent of schools for many years, I know the importance of team-building. The following people have played an important part in the publication and marketing of this book: Sara Fortenberry, Bill Robison, Brenda White, Susan Coker, Lori Quinn, Belinda Bass, and Lori Gliko. I would especially like to thank everyone at Oliver-Nelson Books: Victor Oliver, Rose Marie Sroufe, Brian Hampton, Esther Fitzpatrick, Todd Ross, and Marie Sennett.

It is my hope that, collectively, we will prevent individuals from becoming victims of grasshopper mentality and instead teach and inspire them to become giant slayers.

INTRODUCTION

God Had *Somebody* in Mind

According to an old legend, God first created birds without wings. Later, He put wings down beside them and said, "Now, I want you to pick up your identity and wear it."

Some birds objected and refused to pick up their wings. It was not long before those birds were killed by other animals, since they were slow moving on foot.

Other birds decided to pick up their wings and carry them around on their shoulders. At first, the wings seemed heavy. However, as they got used to them, the wings seemed to grow into their bodies. The birds began to experiment with their now-attached wings, flapping them this way and that. And as you can guess, a few of them took off. Other birds quickly caught on, and soon, an entire flock was soaring toward the clouds.

For more than thirty years as an educator—a coach, a teacher, a principal, a superintendent of schools—I have watched young people as well as my fellow teachers struggle to pick up their identities and, eventually, to soar with success in being who they were created to be.

The fact is that each of us was created to be *somebody.* We were created to pick up our identities and soar. God had a master plan in mind when He created this world, and He had a role planned for each of us at our creation. What may seem to you today to be a burden, a disability, a deficit, a problem, or an impossibility may actually be your wings!

We are very title conscious as a people. For years, I saw myself as a string of titles—coach, teacher, principal, superintendent, speaker, foundation president. At home, I saw myself as husband, father, and now grandfather. The Lord calls each of us to be a friend, not a title. In being the Lord's friends, we become good and faithful servants, willing to do and be what He wants us to do and be. And what the Lord wants for each of us is to become the *somebody* He created each of us to be.

The Lord made you with a set of fingerprints that are unique. Nobody else has them. Only you. The same goes for the prints of your feet, your palms, your voice, and your genetic code. You are *somebody* unique with a never-before-made body.

The Lord made you with a history that nobody else has. He put you in a distinctive time and place in history, and He has given you a one-of-a-kind sequence and series of experiences in your life. You are *somebody* unique with a never-before-lived past, present, and future.

The Lord made you with a set of abilities, talents, gifts, and potentialities that nobody else has in precisely the same combination and degree. He has given you opportunities to develop those innate gifts. He has given you interests and desires and dreams that are solely your own. You are *somebody* unique with a never-before-realized potential.

The Lord made you for good. He designed you with good in mind. He said, "It is good," when you were born. He desires that you live your life in health and spiritual wholeness, having your needs met. His greatest hope is that you will make the right choices in your life so that you can live with Him for all eternity.

The Lord has given you the potential for glory—splendor and luster and light to your life that reflect His glory.

The poet, essayist, and gracious southern gentleman Archibald Rutledge once wrote a lovely story about a man named Sam, the engineer of a tugboat on a lazy South Carolina river named the Santee.

In Dr. Rutledge's opinion, the engine room of a tiny tugboat on a lazy river is just about the worst abode known to civilized people. The odors from kitchen, smokestack, and engine all seemed to congregate in the engine room. Dr. Rutledge often crossed the river on the tugboat nicknamed *The Foam,* but each time he did, the sights and smells as he passed the engine room almost made him ill. The grease, slime, and grime were repulsive to him.

One memorable day he climbed aboard and saw a new engineer, Sam, sitting in the doorway of the engine room reading his Bible as he waited for the passengers to come aboard. Sam was immaculate in person and in dress. Rutledge noticed a strange splendor of wisdom in his eyes—in his countenance, the evidence of peace with God, himself, the world, and yes, even the engine room. Looking beyond Sam, Rutledge saw beauty! The brasses of the engine room shone. The bilge water was gone, as were the filth, the stench, and the grime. Clothes, brooms, mops, and tools were all in place. The engine room had become a place of order. Rutledge was amazed at the transformation.

He asked Sam about whether it was a new tug. Sam assured him it was the same old boat. He asked if the engine was new. Sam replied that it was the same old engine. Rutledge asked, "How on earth and water did this transformation come about?"

Sam's answer was classic. "Mister," he said, "it's just this way: I got a glory."

Sam had the inner glow inside him of knowing who he was, not only what he was gifted to do, but for whom he was to use his gifts. He knew his purpose and place in life, but also the One who had given him purpose and place.

Sam had the inner glory of knowing that he was *somebody* connected to the supreme *Somebody.*

And yet, so few people know this.

One philosopher has estimated that 95 percent of all the people in the world live according to what their bodies tell them. They live from fleshly desire to desire, scrambling to eat when they are hungry, sleep when they are exhausted, and drink when they are thirsty.

Only five out of a hundred live according to what they think and believe in their minds. And four out of those five think and believe what others tell them to think and believe. They rarely step beyond the group norm, the peer opinion, the general train of thought. Only 1 percent of the people truly think and believe what the Lord has said to them about themselves and about their unique purpose and place on this earth.

Of those who hear God's unique call, only about one in ten will actually *act* on the distinctive role in life and seek to fulfill it.

Of those who seek to fulfill their destinies, only one in a thousand will actually be courageous enough to stand up to each giant and overcome it successfully in the power and authority of faith.

When you work out these percentages mathematically, you can quickly conclude that only one in a million will strive with full intent and courage to become the unique *somebody* that person was created and destined to be! And yet, each of us was destined at birth to be a one-in-a-million person. There is no set formula for determining which baby will grab hold of his or her destiny and pursue it, which person will become a giant slayer.

Giant slayers aren't limited to any one class . . . age . . . sex . . . nationality . . . race . . . location . . . IQ level . . . or any other singularly defining characteristic. The vast majority of the truly outstanding people in history have come from nondescript or troublesome backgrounds, have lived in tumultuous ages, and have overcome incredible obstacles.

Furthermore, giant slayers rarely follow a particular course of study, earn a particular degree, attend a particular school, or learn a particular body of knowledge. Giant slayers exist in every walk of life and arise in every profession and circumstance.

What keeps people from becoming their best?

In my opinion, it is grasshopper mentality. Grasshopper mentality is an inner disease of the spirit. It's hardly ever diagnosed, and yet it is rampant.

Most of us know all the warning signs of the major killer diseases of our time. We can quickly list the telltale symptoms of cancer, heart disease, diabetes, AIDS, and other major ailments that too often are named a cause of death.

We also are becoming quite adept at labeling psychological and sociological flaws and faults. The terms *ADD, codependency, abuse,* and *addict* have all taken on new meaning in just the last two or three decades. We are learning more and more about how to treat people who have experienced terrible trauma in their lives.

But few of us know that we have grasshopper mentality, and those who suspect they do rarely know what to do about it.

Overcoming grasshopper mentality means you are willing to pick up your wings and become the *somebody* you were created to be.

Thinking like a giant slayer means that you are willing to develop an inner glory and let it infect, impact, and illuminate every area of your life. Winning in the land of giants is what this book is all about.

CHAPTER 1

What Is Grasshopper Mentality?

The phrase "grasshopper mentality" is drawn from a statement made by a group of spies whom Moses sent to scout out Canaan, the Land of Promise.

Twelve spies were sent into the land with this command from Moses:

> Go up this way into the South, and go up to the mountains, and see what the land is like: whether the people who dwell in it are strong or weak, few or many; whether the land they dwell in is good or bad; whether the cities they inhabit are like camps or strongholds; whether the land is rich or poor; and whether there are forests there or not. Be of good courage. And bring some of the fruit of the land (Num. 13:17–20).

The spies did as they were told, and for forty days, they surveyed the land. When they came to the Valley of Eshcol, they cut down a branch with one cluster of grapes as evidence of the fruit of the land. The cluster of grapes was so large they had to carry it on a pole between two men!

When the spies returned and gave their report, they had only good to say about the land itself. "It truly flows with milk and honey," they reported. They all agreed that the cities were fortified and large, and that the people were strong. When it came to the facts of their report, they were in agreement.

Then Caleb, one of the spies sent by Moses, said, "Let us go up at once and take possession, for we are well able to overcome it." Joshua, another of the spies, agreed with him.

The other ten men, however, had a different opinion. This is what they said:

> We are not able to go up against the people, for they are stronger than we. . . . The land through which we have gone as spies is a land that devours its inhabitants, and all the people whom we saw in it are men of great stature. There we saw the giants (the descendants of Anak came from the giants); and we were like grasshoppers in our own sight, and so we were in their sight (Num. 13:31–33).

Like grasshoppers in our own sight, and so we were in their sight.

That's a grasshopper mentality.

And as is so often the case, the grasshopper mentality prevailed.

MOSES ALSO A VICTIM!

Why didn't Moses, one of the greatest leaders in all of history, sway the multitudes to see the situation as Caleb and Joshua saw it rather than as the ten intimidated spies?

Could it be that Moses had also suffered from grasshopper mentality?

One day as Moses was tending the flocks of his father-in-law on Horeb, called the mountain of God, he encountered the Lord, who called to him from the midst of a bush that was burning with fire but was not consumed. The Lord said, "Behold, the cry of the children of Israel has come to Me, and I have also seen the oppression with which the Egyptians oppress them. Come now, therefore, and I will send you to

Pharaoh that you may bring My people, the children of Israel, out of Egypt."

Moses responded with his own version of grasshopper mentality: "Who am I that I should go to Pharaoh, and that I should bring the children of Israel out of Egypt?" (See Exod. 3:1–11.)

The Lord told Moses that He would be with him. He gave Moses His name, and He told Moses specifically what to say to the children of Israel.

Still, Moses was not convinced: "But suppose they will not believe me or listen to my voice; suppose they say, 'The LORD has not appeared to you.'" (See Exod. 4:1.)

The Lord caused the shepherd's rod in Moses' hand to become a wonder-working rod—one that would turn into a serpent and then become a rod again. He also allowed Moses to experience temporary leprosy when he put his hand in his bosom and then have the leprosy cured just as quickly—both as signs to cause the people to believe. And the Lord told Moses that He would give him the power to turn water into blood as he poured water from a pitcher out onto dry land.

How did Moses reply? "O my Lord, I am not eloquent, neither before nor since You have spoken to Your servant; but I am slow of speech and slow of tongue" (Exod. 4:10).

Again, we see a grasshopper mind-set at work!

The Lord promised to teach Moses what to say. Moses responded yet a third time, "O my Lord, please send by the hand of whomever else You may send" (Exod. 4:13).

A grasshopper mentality, once ingrained, is very difficult to overcome.

■

No one is inherently inferior to another human being.

■

The anger of the Lord kindled against Moses, and He said, "Is not Aaron the Levite your brother? I know that he can speak well. And look, he is also coming out to meet you." The Lord told Moses in no uncertain terms that Aaron *would* speak for him, Moses *would* take the rod in his hand, and Moses *would* do the signs. And it was only as the Lord directly and forcefully commanded Moses to obey that Moses took the rod of God in his hand and returned to Pharaoh to demand that he permit the children of Israel to leave Egypt. (See Exod. 4:14–31.)

Yes, Moses appears to have been a victim of grasshopper mentality. So when the ten spies came back in fear and trembling at the sight of giants in the land, Moses could do little to rally the people against what they said and felt.

■

A grasshopper mentality has to do with a person's perception of himself or herself.

■

And what was the result?

The report of the ten spies filled the people with such fear that they wept and cried all night. When Joshua and Caleb attempted to calm their fears and speak words of optimism and faith to them, the people voiced a desire to stone them to death. The net result was that the children of Israel wandered in a wilderness for forty years—intimidated by the people of Canaan—until all of those who had grasshopper mentality had died. Joshua and Caleb alone were allowed the privilege of going into the Promised Land and eventually conquering it, as they had believed all along they were destined to do.

AN ABIDING SENSE OF INFERIORITY

A grasshopper mentality is an abiding feeling of being inferior in the presence of another person. No one is inherently inferior to another human being. But some people feel inferior to others or think they are inferior. This grasshopper mentality causes a person to

- focus on his weaknesses instead of his strengths, and on his limitations rather than his potential.
- become negative in her appraisal of herself, even in the presence of positive facts.

- limit his attempts at success—to stop short of taking risks that might lead him to greatness, to avoid the opportunities afforded by new challenges.
- to sell herself short.

A grasshopper mentality is a pervasive opinion of oneself as being unworthy, with lesser value, of little regard. As an opinion, grasshopper mentality may or may not be rooted in fact and reality.

That's why even highly successful people can feel intimidated and have a grasshopper mentality. A grasshopper mentality has to do with a person's perception of himself or herself. It is a subjective appraisal, not an objective one.

EVEN HIGHLY SUCCESSFUL PEOPLE CAN SUFFER FROM GRASSHOPPER MENTALITY

One of the most positive, optimistic people in our century admitted to having had a grasshopper mentality as a young man. Dr. Norman Vincent Peale wrote in *The True Joy of Positive Living:*

> Perhaps the most difficult problem I ever faced as a youth was my consummate inferiority complex. I was shy and filled with self-doubt. In fact, I lived like a scared rabbit. I constantly told myself that I had no brains, no ability, that I didn't amount to anything and never would. I lived in a miserable world of self-deprecation. Then I became aware that people were agreeing with me, for it is a fact that others will unconsciously take you at your own self-appraisal.

Winston Churchill admitted to feelings of inferiority and low self-esteem. So did former President Lyndon B. Johnson, who admitted to feeling inferior to his Cabinet members who had graduated from Harvard University—he himself being a graduate from Southwest Texas State University.

Just look around you, and you'll find that nearly everyone

you meet is suffering from grasshopper mentality in at least one relationship or in one area in life. This way of thinking is epidemic in our culture. It's everywhere! In fact, I suspect it's a worldwide phenomenon. Educators from Africa, Germany, Belgium, Australia, Switzerland, and Canada have personally told me of their being victims of this epidemic, and of others they know who are leading miserable lives as a result of grasshopper mentality.

Once you start questioning people about what makes them feel low, what frightens them, who intimidates them, you quickly discover that the majority of people in our society seem to be grasshopper-thinking people! The famous Henry David Thoreau statement may well be more accurate than ever: "The mass of men lead lives of quiet desperation."

And what is the result of a pervasive grasshopper mentality in a culture?

First, important cultural institutions become infected with a "we can't, they can" attitude—from the military to schools, churches to businesses, homes to government bodies, prisons to welfare offices. We end up with conclusions that are rooted in an opinion of intimidation rather than an opinion of strength and victory:

- The Japanese and the Germans seem to have figured out the new business protocols for the coming age of global expansion. We haven't. We may never catch up and lead again!
- The street gangs are taking over. Crime is on the rise. What impact can a hardworking, law-abiding citizen have?
- The economy is out of control. Nobody seems to have a handle on the deficit. Perhaps nothing can be done.
- The disease is rampant. There's no cure and probably won't be. The best a person can do is hope he doesn't contract it.
- Rehabilitation doesn't work. A criminal is a criminal is a criminal. All we can do is keep 'em locked up.

- The welfare cycle goes from one generation to the next. Once people get trapped into the system, it's nearly impossible for them to find a way out.

A defeatist attitude is pervasive. We tend to walk about wringing our hands with an "Oh, what can we do?" attitude rather than taking charge and tackling problems head-on. We, in essence, wander in a wilderness of our own making— going in circles around a problem rather than overcoming it in a definitive, strong, decisive way.

Second, the individuals with a grasshopper mentality frequently feel exhausted, both emotionally and physically, from wandering without goals and direction against their enemies and wondering who might pummel them emotionally at the next bend of the road. You don't have to look very far to see people who are suffering from "wandering, wondering" behaviors. Depression, suicide attempts, and drug and alcohol abuse—obvious outward manifestations of these inner feelings—are all on the increase in our society despite our attempts to tell one another, "I'm okay. You're okay."

■ *Adults* can *redirect the thought life!* ■

Is there any hope?

Yes!

GRASSHOPPER MENTALITY CAN BE OVERCOME!

We need not struggle with feeling intimidated by people or situations. It *is* possible to live as Philippians 4:13 admonishes: "I can do all things through Christ who strengthens me."

Part of the solution comes in recognizing the problem, choosing to confront it, and realizing that what we once learned as children may not have been correct. Dr. R. Buckminster Fuller, inventor of the geodesic dome, once said,

Man starts at birth with one hundred percent potential and the only way he is altered is in a negative way, which detracts from his maximum realization. Scientific studies prove that fifty percent of man's alterability, in a negative way, occurs between birth and four years old. If the trust of a child is betrayed before he is four, that child is almost certain to be a school dropout or have a low I.Q.

Beyond facing up to what we may have incorrectly internalized as children, we must take active steps toward replacing our attitudes of inferiority, insecurity, and inadequacy with positive beliefs and behaviors on a daily basis.

Adults *can* redirect the thought life! No person needs to be tormented or limited by an intimidation complex throughout life.

In addition to reversing a grasshopper mentality in ourselves as adults, we must make a conscious effort as caring parents, teachers, grandparents, and adult role models to avoid creating a grasshopper mentality in our children. We must reverse the trend in our own lives and in our culture as a whole. The time has come to train a new generation of giant slayers, not grasshopper thinkers!

Today is the day to start.

CHAPTER 2

Thinking
Like
a Giant Slayer

When we think of giant slayers and giants, nearly all of us think immediately of David and Goliath.

Goliath certainly qualified as a giant physically. He was "six cubits and a span" tall, which by our best estimates is about nine feet tall. He wore a coat of armor that weighed two hundred pounds, not counting the bronze armor on his legs. The iron spearhead on his spear weighed twenty-five pounds, and the spear itself was described as being like a "weaver's beam." Goliath was one mountain of a man.

Goliath was also a giant in his reputation. He was considered a "champion" of the Philistines. We don't know what Goliath did to earn that title and reputation, but we can guess how the people must have treated him because of the way we treat our champions today. We look upon world-class boxers and weight lifters and wrestlers with awe. We look upon our ace pilots and military heroes with respect. And we say, "If I need to be defended by anybody, let it be that person!"

That's the way the Philistines treated Goliath. They sent him out into the valley that stood between the Philistine army and the armies of King Saul, and they said, "This man represents our best hope of victory."

Out in that plain, Goliath marched back and forth for forty days, coming out every morning and every evening to taunt Israel. He would cry,

> Choose a man for yourselves, and let him come down to me. If he is able to fight with me and kill me, then we will be your servants. But if I prevail against him and kill him, then you shall be our servants and serve us. . . . I defy the armies of Israel this day; give me a man, that we may fight together (1 Sam. 17:8–10).

Most important, Goliath was a giant in the minds and hearts of Saul and all his soldiers. We are told that when Goliath bellowed out his threats and taunts, the Israelites "were dismayed and greatly afraid" (1 Sam. 17:11).

All except one man. David. The youngest of eight sons born to Jesse.

Can you imagine yourself the youngest of eight boys in a family? That's definitely a position we might describe as the low man on the totem pole. Can you imagine what those older brothers thought of David? In their minds, he no doubt was the baby of the family, the little kid. David grew up overlooked and probably ignored for the most part, except for the fact that one day, a man had come into his life and had said, "This is the one." That man had been the prophet Samuel, who had come to Jesse's house at God's order and had anointed David with oil in the midst of his brothers.

Initially, David wasn't even included in the serious business of a family sacrifice and holy service of consecration. Instead, he was sent out to watch the sheep. It was only after all of the other brothers had appeared before Samuel and had been told, "Neither has the LORD chosen this one," that Jesse admitted that he had another son, his youngest, out in the fields.

Samuel knew that he was anointing David to one day be king of Israel, but there is no indication that David, Jesse, or any of the brothers knew that at the time. They only knew that Samuel, through the LORD, had chosen David. (See 1 Sam. 16:1–13.)

David certainly wasn't a giant of a man in his brothers' eyes when he arrived in their military camp one day at the request of his father. The three oldest sons of Jesse had followed Saul to battle, and Jesse had sent David to take them a sack of dried grain and some loaves of bread, and to bring back news of their welfare.

David arrived in the camp just as Goliath was getting ready for his morning strut up and down in the valley. He rushed out with his brothers to hear Goliath roar at the army of Israel. He saw how the men of Israel cowered in front of Goliath and retreated to their original position, "dreadfully afraid."

David was appalled. He said, "Who is this uncircumcised Philistine, that he should defy the armies of the living God?" And when he heard that there was a great reward for whoever might take on Goliath, David asked, "What shall be done for the man who kills this Philistine and takes away the reproach from Israel?" (1 Sam. 17:26).

David wasn't yet a winner in the land of giants, but he was *thinking* like a winner!

And as he went from group to group of soldiers asking the same questions, trying to rouse them to action, he began to stir up the men. On the one hand, he encouraged them to defeat Goliath because Goliath was an evil enemy who deserved to be defeated. On the other hand, he encouraged them to kill Goliath because there was a reward to be gained. He used the same motivational techniques that coaches have used for years in preparing their teams for a big game: "These guys deserve to be beaten by you because you are the better team," and "Do it for the home school and for the championship ring!"

David's brothers tried to stop him from thinking and talking like a giant slayer. One of his brothers, Eliab, said in essence, "Why are you daring us to fight this guy? Do you just want to see us go out and get killed?" Eliab definitely was a victim of grasshopper mentality.

David answered, "What have I done now? Is there not a cause?"

As much as he tried to encourage the soldiers to take on Goliath, the only person that David truly encouraged was himself. He finally said to Saul, "Let no man's heart fail because of him; your servant will go and fight with this Philistine."

Even Saul was a victim of grasshopper mentality at that point. He said, "You are not able." He pointed to David's youth and inexperience as a soldier.

■

Win the battle, and the rewards can be great.

■

David replied with giant-slaying fervor, "Your servant has killed both lion and bear; and this uncircumcised Philistine will be like one of them, seeing he has defied the armies of the living God."

Finally, Saul gave permission for David to give it a try, and he loaned him his own armor. David put it on and then immediately took it off. It didn't fit. (See 1 Sam. 17:29–39.)

David knew who he was. He was a shepherd, the son of Jesse, an Israelite, a chosen child of God, and a man anointed by the prophet. He knew the Spirit of the Lord was with him. He also believed that God was on the side of Israel. David knew that he was *somebody* and that he was associated with *Somebody* bigger than Goliath.

A WINNER IN THE LAND OF GIANTS KNOWS WHO HE IS

The person who is a winner in the land of giants inevitably carries these same traits as David:

- He knows who he is in the Lord; she knows that she is a child of God.
- She knows that she has a divine destiny; he knows he has been chosen by the Lord.

- He knows that God is greater than any giant he can face; she knows that she can conquer any problem with the Lord on her side.
- She knows that to slay the giant before her, she must be 100 percent herself; he knows he can't take on the identity of another person and hope to win.

David took his staff to help him get down the mountain to the plain, and once down by the brook, he chose five smooth stones from it and put them in a pouch. He had his sling in his other hand.

As David got closer to Goliath, Goliath began to roar at him in disdain, "Am I a dog, that you come to me with sticks? . . . Come to me, and I will give your flesh to the birds of the air and the beasts of the field!" (1 Sam. 17:43–44).

David shouted back at Goliath. As far as we know, he was the only one who ever did. And he didn't mince words:

> You come to me with a sword, with a spear, and with a javelin. But I come to you in the name of the LORD of hosts, the God of the armies of Israel, whom you have defied. This day the LORD will deliver you into my hand, and I will strike you and take your head from you. And this day I will give the carcasses of the camp of the Philistines to the birds of the air and the wild beasts of the earth, that all the earth may know that there is a God in Israel. Then all this assembly shall know that the LORD does not save with sword and spear; for the battle is the LORD's, and He will give you into our hands (1 Sam. 17:45–47).

Notice that David didn't talk only about himself as Goliath had. He talked about himself *and the Lord*. David wasn't going out to meet Goliath in his own strength or trusting in his own weapons or abilities. He was trusting in God.

Goliath started toward David, and David ran toward Goliath. He may very well have been the only person who ever ran toward Goliath.

As he ran, David loaded his slingshot with a stone and

slung it with great force at the vulnerable bare spot in Goliath's armor—the area just above his eyes and below his helmet. He hit his mark. The stone was moving with such velocity that it sunk into Goliath's forehead when it struck him. David's aim was perfect. Goliath fell forward on his face. Two points at the buzzer. A touchdown in the final second of the game!

David realized, however, the probability that Goliath was only stunned and not dead. He knew the moment had come for finishing off his enemy, but he had no sword. Perhaps the most dramatic and courageous moment lay ahead. David needed to move toward his only stunned victim and remove his sword from its sheath. Unencumbered and moving swiftly, David pulled Goliath's own sword and beheaded Goliath with it.

Giant slayers today also exhibit these traits of David:

- They shout back positively when the world shouts negatively at them.
- They run toward their enemy giants, seeing them as challenges to be conquered.
- They hit their mark, doing what they know to do with all of their ability.
- They finish the job, completely and definitively.

When Goliath fell, his colleagues fled. The Philistines took off for Ekron, and the army of Saul, roused into action, followed them and slaughtered them. The victory was complete. And David won his reward—not only the armor of Goliath as a trophy, but the praise of Israel and, eventually, the hand of King Saul's daughter.

As the old saying goes, "No battle, no spoils." Win the battle, however, and the rewards can be great.

Winners in the land of giants not only defeat the enemies that taunt them but also win rewards for themselves in the process.

PREPARING TO THINK LIKE A WINNER
IN THE LAND OF GIANTS

David killed a giant in a morning. But he didn't become a giant slayer in his heart in a day.

Getting to the point where you think like a giant slayer is a process. It takes time. And often, we are given an opportunity to face medium-sized giants before we face truly large ones.

That was certainly true in David's life. David had defeated both bears and lions before he ever encountered Goliath. A bear or a lion was no less deadly than the giant Goliath. In some ways, those enemies may have been more deadly since they were as agile and swift as David.

■

How has God prepared you for winning in the land of giants?

■

What is important to note is that David had been trained as a shepherd. Part of a shepherd's training included learning what to do when a wild animal attacked the flock. David was on the alert for lions and bears in his role as a shepherd. David had experience in expecting lions and bears, just as he had experience in fighting them. He had developed courage over time, not in an instant or as a result of one or two experiences. David's entire pattern of thinking was of defense of the flock and offense against enemy attackers.

The mind-set that David had gained in anticipating, facing, and defeating wild predators out in the fields stood him in good stead when he faced Goliath. In many ways, Goliath was only a larger and more thoroughly armed predator attempting to ravage a larger flock—the flock of God's people.

David also had experience with a slingshot. That kind of experience takes daily practice. No doubt David had spent countless hours slinging stones at inanimate objects and perhaps even a few scurrying rodents or fluttering birds. David's first try at using a slingshot wasn't in the valley where he faced Goliath. He was well prepared for that moment, knowing how to choose stones of just the right shape, weight, and size, and how to load those stones in his slingshot on the run. David had gained confidence in himself that he could handle a slingshot, and he also had the faith that God could use his well-developed skills for His glory.

How has God prepared you for winning in the land of giants?

In all likelihood, you can point to times in your past in which God has allowed you to gain experience and small victories that have prepared you for the challenges you face today. Think about those past victories. What did you learn through them? What skills do you have now because of them?

■

Success builds upon success.

■

Every teacher knows that the best way to help a student is to move her just one step from what she knows to what she doesn't know. Education is a process of building upon a foundation of previous learning. If a student misses part of the foundation, she will have trouble grasping new concepts that require that information or skill. If a student doesn't have a prerequisite, she will have trouble grasping the new concept.

Rarely are we asked to face giants cold. We nearly always have at least some of the foundation we need in place, and we nearly always have access to those who can help us fill in the foundational gaps if we have them. Furthermore, the Bible promises us that we never face giants alone as long as we trust in the Lord.

GOD DOESN'T DESIRE
THAT WE BE MAULED

I once heard Coach Joe Paterno, head coach at Penn State and one of the best ever, on a radio talk show. The host of the show was trying to get Coach Paterno to criticize other coaches who have more flamboyant styles and tempers than he has. Coach Paterno refused to engage in the criticism, stating that he, too, had made mistakes in dealing with his players. He then related the following incident.

A young freshman football player had come to Pennsylvania State with an excellent reputation. He had been highly recruited. Coach Paterno and his staff decided to see just how tough the young player was, so on the first day of practice, they assigned the freshman the task of blocking one of the seniors. They picked the meanest, toughest senior they had. In fact, that particular senior went on to star as a professional defensive end. The attempted blocking assignment took place in full view of all the coaches and players.

The freshman was completely run over by the senior. After four or five devastating square-offs, the coaches called off the massacre.

The freshman never came back to another practice. He left the school, and Penn State lost a potential star. More important, Coach Paterno felt as if he personally had a hand in destroying the young man's self-image by forcing him to participate in a situation in which the great likelihood was that he would fail. Paterno concluded that he should have placed the player in a situation where he could have been successful. He claimed it was one of his worst mistakes as a coach.

Coach Paterno was saying, in essence, that he should have given the young player a lion or a bear to slay. He should have eased him up to the challenge of facing a Goliath.

Success builds upon success. When we catch hold of that concept, we find ourselves thinking in relationship to others, *What can I do to help this person succeed in this moment, in this assignment, in this course, in this endeavor, in this venture, in accomplishing this goal?* The goal may be a small one, and indeed, it should be a small one if it is the first goal in a new field or a new area of skill.

When it comes to our own lives, we are wise to take on challenges that are just beyond our present capabilities and level of success. If we shoot too high as a first step, we have a much greater likelihood of failure. Our ultimate goal may be the moon and stars, but as a step toward that goal, we need to be realistic and take on lions and bears before we take on Goliaths.

The Bible speaks repeatedly of our ability to grow as human beings. In 1 John 4:17, we find a statement about the ability of our love to grow: "And as we live with Christ, our love grows more perfect and complete" (TLB).

Elsewhere in God's Word, we are admonished to grow in faith, grow in our ability to care for others, grow up in Christ, and grow to become fully mature in the Lord. As we grow, we are transformed, changed, renewed in our minds by the Holy Spirit. We become bigger and better in the Lord the more we diligently seek after Him, invite His presence into our lives, study His Word, and stay in constant contact with Him.

What is true for all areas of spiritual growth is true for transformation from being a person with grasshopper mentality to being a person who thinks like a giant slayer. We grow and change, and as part of that process, we are prepared to take on bigger and bigger giants—and win. Our resolve to do so also grows. We not only think like winners in the land of giants, but we become winners in reality!

Expect your ability to think like a winner in the land of giants to grow over time and with each new experience. Expect to get to the point eventually where you automatically say to yourself and others, "We can take this giant."

ROOTING YOUR THOUGHTS IN FAITH

David voiced no doubts that he could take on Goliath and win. In fact, he didn't even hedge his efforts by saying, "If the Lord is with me," or "If this be God's will," or "Should the Lord desire." David knew who he was. David knew who God was to him, and to his people, and what God had promised to do for them if they obeyed and trusted Him. David knew without any doubt that Goliath was an enemy who needed to be defeated. David knew that he was going to win the confrontation with the giant.

He believed it for others and no doubt would have gladly cheered on another person in the defeat of Goliath.

David saw anybody who was willing to go against Goliath

with all faith placed in God and without any doubt left over as a person destined for victory.

In other words, David's giant-slaying thinking wasn't limited to himself and his confrontation with Goliath. It extended to all areas of his life. It was something he believed strongly as part of his faith in God.

Thinking like a winner in the land of giants isn't rooted in our ability. It is rooted in our faith. Our faith relates to God. When we think that we are able to take on giants and win, we are actually thinking that we *and God* can take on a particular giant and win. We have the ability to take on the giant and emerge victorious because we have the belief that God is with us and in us and He desires to work through us. To think like a giant slayer is to have an active faith in God. It is to see ourselves as part of God's army, doing God's work on this earth, and fulfilling God's purpose for our lives even as He extends His kingdom.

If we think we can slay giants in our own ability and strength, we are sorely mistaken, and we are presumptuous. Most giants will swallow us alive if we face them strictly on our own. We are no match for evil. We are no match for those who are filled with or motivated by evil.

But as the apostle Paul wrote to the Romans, "If God is for us, who can be against us?" (Rom. 8:31). If we are fighting giants who are coming against us as His children and against His people and His purpose, He will be on our side. Who can withstand God's assault?

Did you ever see the movie *The Bear*? In one of the funniest and most inspiring scenes of that movie, a young bear cub stands up on his hind legs and seems both amused and proud when a stalking mountain cat slinks away from him in fear. What we see, but what the cub doesn't see, is his giant papa bear standing up on his hind legs just behind the cub.

We have the privilege to think like a giant slayer, act like a giant slayer, and then actually slay giants because standing just behind us is the Giant Slayer, the Lord Jesus Christ Himself, the Captain of our army and the Victor eternal and supreme.

CALEB TOOK THE MOUNTAIN!

Although we often think of David as the famous giant slayer of the Bible, the first giant slayer was actually Caleb. Caleb was one of the two spies who went into Canaan and returned saying,

> If the LORD delights in us, then He will bring us into this land and give it to us. . . . Only do not rebel against the LORD, nor fear the people of the land, for they are our bread; their protection has departed from them, and the LORD is with us. Do not fear them (Num. 14:8–9).

As far as we know, Caleb and Joshua were the only two men who survived the forty years of wandering in the wilderness and were allowed to enter the Land of Promise. Their faith in God's ability to give them the land never wavered, and neither did their obedience in following the Lord.

After much of the land of Canaan had been taken by the Israelites under the leadership of Joshua, the children of Judah came to Gilgal. Caleb made a bold request of Joshua:

> You know the word which the LORD said to Moses the man of God concerning you and me in Kadesh Barnea. I was forty years old when Moses the servant of the LORD sent me from Kadesh Barnea to spy out the land, and I brought back word to him as it was in my heart. Nevertheless my brethren who went up with me made the heart of the people melt, but I wholly followed the LORD my God. So Moses swore on that day, saying, "Surely the land where your foot has trodden shall be your inheritance and your children's forever, because you have wholly followed the LORD my God." And now, behold, the LORD has kept me alive, as He said, these forty-five years, ever since the LORD spoke this word to Moses while Israel wandered in the wilderness; and now, here I am this day, eighty-five years old. As yet I am as strong this day as on the day that Moses sent me; just as my strength was then, so now is my strength for war, both for going out and for coming in. Now therefore, give me this mountain of which the LORD

spoke in that day; for you heard in that day how the Anakim were there, and that the cities were great and fortified. It may be that the LORD will be with me, and I shall be able to drive them out as the LORD said (Josh. 14:6–12).

Caleb asked that the mountain of the giants, the Anakim, be given to him as an inheritance. Caleb was still ready and willing to take on the giants. Talk about a giant-slaying attitude! Caleb didn't have one ounce of grasshopper mentality as he made his bold request of Joshua.

Caleb hadn't wavered in his belief that God wanted His people to possess Canaan.

Caleb hadn't wavered in his confidence that with God's help, he could take on any giant and win.

Caleb didn't use any excuses. Even at eighty-five, he considered himself able to win the victory.

Joshua blessed Caleb and gave him Hebron as an inheritance for his family. The name of Hebron was originally Kirjath-arba. Arba was the name of the great man among the Anakim. Hebron was the headquarters city of the giants. In other words, Caleb took on the giant of the giants. He captured it and turned it into his own city.

When David became king, he made his first capital in Hebron. It was only fitting that a giant slayer should want to dwell in a city once occupied by giants but captured by a giant slayer!

A great principle about giant-slaying thinking is evident: the victory of one winner very often inspires another winner. Caleb's victory over the Anakim no doubt inspired David. David's victory inspired the entire army of Saul to pursue the Philistines and win not only the battle, but the war. Your victories over the giants you face will inspire the faith of others to believe for victories in their lives. Not only will you be built up as a person, but the entire body of Christ will be made stronger by your example.

If you want to start thinking like a winner in the land of giants, associate with others who also believe in rejecting grasshopper mentality and embracing a can-do, we-can-take-the-mountain, God-is-on-our-side attitude.

CHAPTER 3

Winning
the Battles of
Each Day

Read the newspaper. Watch television. Talk and listen to people.

It doesn't take long to become mindful that people everywhere are fighting numerous and diverse battles on a daily basis. Nearly everyone you encounter is struggling to overcome something—to deal with and to win a battle against some type of problem that, to a greater or lesser extent, is defeating, intimidating, or overwhelming.

The Chinese symbol for the word *crisis* actually has two interpretations. It can be interpreted as "opportunity" or "problem." A person with a grasshopper mentality would no doubt think *problem* when looking at the symbol. A person with a positive can-do attitude would think *opportunity*. In many situations, the attitude with which we approach a challenge primarily determines whether we will succeed or fail.

THE BATTLEGROUND IS THE MIND

After I made a presentation in Madison, Wisconsin, two women from the audience came forward and shared with me that they were battling cancer. They were in a fight for their lives. Cancer was their giant, and their battle against cancer was an exhaustive one, mentally, emotionally, and physically. Both told me that their oncologists had informed them that 90 percent of their chance of winning the battle over cancer depended on their ability to control their thoughts.

Others have told me of their daily struggle against AIDS, heart disease, and other life-threatening ailments. Again and again, they tell me of the importance of a positive attitude in giving them a good quality of life and hope for the future.

For millions of parents living in poverty across our nation and around the world, feeding and clothing their children are daily battles. The greatest antidote for poverty is not a ration of rice or a dollar for a sandwich; it's hope that tomorrow might be better, that a new opportunity will emerge, that life can be more than an eked-out existence.

Others are battling to keep their marriages together, to become employed or stay employed, and to keep their spirits from being broken by those who seem intent on destroying them psychologically and emotionally. Their battles are mostly battles in their thought lives—battles to keep their self-esteem high, their outlook cheerful, and their spirits strong.

All of these battles against circumstances and situations that are potentially defeating are fought—and must be fought—on a daily basis in the arena of one's thought life. The war itself may have been ongoing for some time, and it may continue for days, weeks, months, and perhaps even years into the future. The hand-to-hand combat—or in this case, the thought-to-thought combat—happens in each twenty-four-hour period. It is in the battle of the day that we must face and defeat our enemies of fear, discouragement, and failure.

AS A MAN THINKS, SO IS HE

Proverbs 23:7 gives us centuries-old advice about human nature and the battleground of the mind: "As he thinks in his heart, so is he." Each of us, no doubt, can point to examples of that proverb in action. For me, one of the prime examples of this truth has been in the life of my beautiful granddaughter, Michelle.

Even though I've passed my sixtieth birthday, I still have a full head of hair. Perhaps for that reason, I have never given much thought about having hair or not having hair. All that changed in September of 1992. Michelle, the apple of her Pap Pap's eye, began to lose her hair. It was frightening to all of us. Over a four-month period, she lost 75 percent of her beautiful naturally curly blonde hair.

Several dermatologists diagnosed Michelle as having *alopecia areata,* which means simply "hair loss." They didn't know what caused it or how to treat it. Very little is known about the condition, and less than 1 percent of the population falls victim to it. The condition apparently involves the interaction of the autonomic nervous system and the immune system. To the best of the doctors' knowledge, Michelle's immune system began attacking her hair follicles.

The students in Michelle's class at school were shocked, inquisitive, and at times cruel in asking Michelle why she was losing her hair. In restaurants people would often stare at us, and occasionally, a well-meaning person would ask, "Is she undergoing chemotherapy?"

One morning as I was driving Michelle to school, she told me that she had awakened in the middle of the night worrying about losing her eyelashes and eyebrows, since the doctor had told her that was a possibility. As she told me of her concern, I thought my heart would burst with sadness.

We began to stress to Michelle that she had to make a conscious decision every day to fill her mind with positive thoughts that she was going to overcome alopecia areata, and to believe God to restore her hair.

We continued to try various treatments recommended by dermatologists. After six months, we returned to her local dermatologist, who examined Michelle and told us that after looking at her hair follicles under a microscope, he was encouraged to see that all of the follicles still seemed to have hair in them, even though one could not see the hair with the naked eye. He then reinforced what we had been saying to Michelle about the importance of positive thinking and faith—of refusing to give in to grasshopper mentality.

The doctor told her about two of his patients with melanoma—a deadly form of skin cancer. He said that one patient's condition was more advanced than the other, but the sicker of the two patients had a positive outlook and, at that time, was winning the battle of the day. He said, "The other patient, whose case is not as advanced, has a helpless, give-up attitude. He's losing the battle."

■

Our first and foremost task is to take control of our thoughts.

■

There is no way to document or chart the impact of faith and a positive attitude on a physical disease—at least not at present—but every physician I've ever met will tell you that there is definitely a link between the two. Medical science has discovered that every thought we think produces a chemical in our bodies. Negative, worrisome thinking produces a chemically unhealthy atmosphere for our cells while positive, loving thoughts create the chemically happy environment our cells need to do their best work of keeping us healthy.

A psychologist a few years ago conducted a study on how people think, and he concluded that those who had more positive thoughts had a much greater likelihood of enjoying the following:

- Better eyesight
- Healthier bodies
- Better bodily function
- Better memory

One of the best-known psychiatrists in our nation, Dr. Karl Menninger, said, "Attitudes are more important than facts."

In the face of no known medical protocol for alopecia areata, perhaps the very best thing Michelle can do is to believe that God will restore her hair! Her positive thinking and faith are the fertile soil in which the various medical treatments can work. Each day, medical miracles are performed, and Michelle's physicians admonish us to keep the faith and to think positively. This advice, of course, would be no mystery to the writers of the Bible.

■
Seek out the positive.
■

The contention is made throughout the Scriptures that the foremost battleground in our victory against our enemies—the circumstances, problems, situations, and people who intimidate us—is the battleground of our minds.

The apostle Paul wrote in 2 Corinthians 10:3–5:

For though we walk in the flesh, we do not war according to the flesh. For the weapons of our warfare are not carnal but mighty in God for pulling down strongholds, *casting down arguments and every high thing that exalts itself against the knowledge of God, bringing every thought into captivity* to the obedience of Christ (emphasis added).

Read some of the other words of wisdom in the Bible about this battle in the mind:

Let this mind be in you which was also in Christ Jesus (Phil. 2:5).

Now your attitudes and thoughts must all be constantly changing for the better (Eph. 4:23 TLB).

Fix your thoughts on what is true and good and right. Think about things that are pure and lovely, and dwell on the fine, good things in others. Think about all you can praise God for and be glad about (Phil. 4:8 TLB).

So watch what you do and what you think (James 2:12 TLB).

Our real challenge in facing battles each day is to decide how we are going to think about those challenges. Our first and foremost task is to take control of our thoughts.

WHICH APPROACH ARE YOU TAKING?

When a person grapples with an intimidating situation or the facts of a negative circumstance loom up into the conscious mind, that person must decide to pursue one of two paths.

Path A calls for the person to

- *curse the problem*. This, in essence, means adding a negative opinion to the negative facts of the situation—in other words, compounding the negativity.
- *nurse the problem*—focusing time and attention on the problem itself rather than on its solution.
- *rehearse the problem*—replaying it repeatedly until the person is actually thinking about very little other than the problem.

I saw this happen in a family I'll call the Andersons. The parents learned that their middle daughter, Angela, was pregnant at eighteen and unmarried. She had no intention of marrying the father of the baby, who, like her, was a freshman at a nearby university.

For several days, the Andersons cursed the problem—wringing their hands at this situation they perceived as being disastrous to their reputation and the future of their daughter. They spent literally dozens of hours nursing the problem—breaking into tears as if they had lost a beloved relative to death. They rehearsed the problem—discussing it from every angle, attempting to analyze what they had done wrong as parents, where they had failed, whether they had any legal recourse against the young man, whether date rape had been involved, what role the university had or had not taken. By the end of two weeks, they were miserable, their daughter was miserable and not speaking to them, and they were totally enveloped by their problem.

They would have done well to take Path B, which calls for a person, upon encountering a negative situation, to

- *disperse it*. A technique used in tackling scientific problems is to break a problem down into its component parts and then to work at each part until an answer is reached. As the component problems are solved, the big problem is also solved. This principle holds true for all of life. One of the most effective things a person can do about what seems to be an overwhelming problem is to attempt to break it down into its smaller component problems and then to deal with the smaller issues one at a time.

- *reverse it*. Seek out the positive. No situation or circumstance is 100 percent bad. There is always some glimmer of hope, some ray of light. Recognize negativity for what it is—a distraction from a positive solution. Dismiss the negativity. Of course, you do not ignore the problem in hopes that it will go away. To the contrary! Disposing of the negative thought means facing the problem *and* facing your negative response, making a conscious decision that the negative response is going to do nothing to solve the problem, and in that light, refusing to dwell on the negative and turning instead to the positive. Only you can reverse the way you feel about a problem.

The Andersons may have chosen to approach the problem with a host of possible solutions, not the least of which would have been to welcome a precious new grandchild into their family and to support their daughter with love and a positive outlook on the future.

A family I'll call the Mettlers took Path B when they learned that their son had not been accepted to any of the five private colleges to which he had applied. They weren't sure who felt the greater disappointment—their son or them. But they realized that their disappointment wasn't going to solve the problem.

They and their son immediately began to map out ways in which they might turn what they perceived as a negative into a positive. They ultimately decided that their son would spend a year—possibly two—at a local community college in an effort to improve his grades and then apply again. Their son also worked part-time, which made the later years at a private college more affordable. When the family looked back four years later, they realized that the path their son had taken was actually a better one than if he had gone away as a freshman to a four-year college.

YOU CAN CHOOSE THE POSITIVE

In 1992, I went to Australia to present workshops on the Power of Positive Students, a systematic program that helps school employees, parents, and students build positive attitudes, virtues, and life skills. I was excited to learn that the students, faculty, and administrators at Palm Beach Currumbin High School in Gold Coast, Australia, had selected this as their slogan for the 1993 school year: "Positive by Choice." Together, they determined to make an effort every day to focus their thoughts and their efforts on the positive things of life (and the positive things in their school), and to do so not as a mandated action but by choice.

> ■
> *You can choose to see the bright side.*
> ■

Their slogan underscores for me what I know to be true in my life and in the lives of hundreds of people with whom I've discussed a grasshopper mentality: you can *choose* to be positive, even in a negative situation.

You can choose to see the bright side.

You can choose to pursue what will bring successful results.

You can choose to look at solutions, answers, and options rather than maintain your focus on the problem.

You can choose to speak a positive word, no matter how dire the circumstance.

You can choose to have courage rather than grasshopper mentality.

POSITIVE THOUGHTS AREN'T PAINFUL!

The story is told of an avid duck hunter who was in the market for a new bird dog. His search ended when he found a dog that would walk on water to retrieve a duck. Shocked by his discovery, the man wondered how he would break this news to his hunting friends. He was sure no one would believe him.

■

Beyond positive thinking is positive doing.

■

The hunter decided to invite a buddy to go with him to see the phenomenon for himself. The two hunters made their way to the blind the next morning and waited. When a team of ducks flew nearby, they shouldered their guns and fired. The dog responded by running across the water and retrieving a bird. The hunter's friend remained silent. He didn't say a word about the amazing dog.

On the drive home, the hunter asked his friend, "Did you notice anything unusual about my new dog?"

"I sure did," responded the friend. "He can't swim."

We can laugh at this little story, but the truth remains that many people are like that hunter's friend. They just hate to say the positive thing. It's as if a positive thought is totally foreign to them. To those people, I want to shout, "A positive thought won't hurt you! It won't cause you pain!"

The fact is, a negative thought is far more likely to cause you pain or to induce situations that result in pain. Consider these statistics:

- Some 70 percent of all adults do not like their jobs. They have a negative opinion about them, and they report that they hate to get up in the morning and go to work. What kind of performance are we likely to expect from these people? Are they the ones most likely to lose their jobs or to have accidents on the job? Are they the most likely to develop work-related ulcers? Is job loss or job-related illness painful? You bet!

- In one survey, psychologists found that up to 80 percent of all the external messages placed daily in the human mind are failure messages—"don't," "can't," and "shouldn't" messages seem to surround us continually, not to mention negative facts about trends, averages, and traffic delays! Those who internalize these messages and personalize them are likely to proceed cautiously. Yet, in worrying so much about being cautious, they are far more likely to end up with serious mental and emotional problems, and to perceive themselves as being failures. Is emotional pain real? Absolutely!
- More than one million young people will drop out of school this year, and the primary reason they will give is this: "I didn't feel valued, wanted, or capable." In other words, they suffer from grasshopper mentality. Is their decision to drop out more likely to cause them financial and social pain? It's inevitable.
- Looking at the dropout problem from another angle—eight out of every ten prisoners are high school dropouts. Nearly all of them admit to their prison counselors that they have felt society was looking down on them long before they committed a crime. Is a life in prison painful? For nearly all prisoners, yes!

Negative thinking can result in pain. But does positive thinking truly help? The evidence is mounting to say that it does. Positive thinking has been shown to release endorphins in the brain, which are the chemicals associated with a feeling of joy and a sense of well-being. These endorphins even block physical pain in the body.

Numerous oncologists and others who treat seriously ill people are advising them to think positively. They are recording longer survival times for those who have faith and a positive attitude.

Positive thinking is not a mere nice idea. It is a perspective on life that is truly helpful to the body, mind, and spirit.

Beyond positive thinking, of course, is positive *doing*. That is the real message of this book. It's not enough for you to think the positive. You must move beyond that to *do* the positive. For example, you can teach your child repeatedly about the principle of honesty and how it is right for a child to be honest. However, it is not until your child begins to act out honesty—to make the honest choice, to exhibit the honest behavior—that the real benefits of honesty are realized in his or her life.

I have asked a number of audience members to come up on stage with me and define the word *positive*. Even young children know that positive is associated with "plus"—that it is something good. The difficulty comes in knowing how to respond positively to life and how to make positive actions and reactions the automatic norm in our lives. Our greatest challenge is not only to think positively but also to respond and act in a positive manner, regardless of the circumstances.

Both our thinking positively and our acting positively begin with our making a choice to think and act in this manner.

MAKING THE CHOICE
FOR THE POSITIVE

In making a choice for the positive, start with these two exercises.

Exercise A: Separating the Positive and the Negative

Take two sheets of paper. Title one "Negative" and the other "Positive." On the sheet headed "Negative," write down three negative thoughts that you think frequently. They may be thoughts about yourself, another person, a situation, your future, or your past. On the sheet headed "Positive," write down three positive attributes or habits you want to acquire and develop.

Now, tear up the sheet labeled "Negative," and throw away all the pieces of paper. Consider yourself to be finished with those thoughts. Take the sheet headed "Positive," and post it someplace—perhaps on a bulletin board, in a binder you open often, on the bathroom mirror, or next to the phone. Remind yourself frequently of the positive attributes or habits you want to develop. The more you put those thoughts into your mind, the more likely you are to act on them. The more you act on them, the more they will become habitual to you. About 95 percent of what we do in a day is out of habit. Make your habits positive!

Exercise B: Replacing Negative Input

Think for a moment about information that you've gained in the last twenty-four hours. Then, write down three or four of the most negative things you've seen, heard, or experienced. What feelings do you have when you think about those things? Are you angry, frustrated, bitter, disappointed, fearful, or upset? Where did you hear those negative statements? What can you do to eliminate the negative from your life? Do you need to turn off the television set awhile? Do you need to tell a negative-speaking friend that you want to discuss positive things?

Now, write down several positive things you've heard or experienced in the last twenty-four hours. What happens when you think about those things? Do you find yourself smiling, feeling contentment and joy, and anticipating tomorrow?

Where did you hear, see, or experience the positive? What more might you do to enhance your opportunities for receiving positive input into your life?

Choose to be a part of the small percentage of all people who take control of their lives—including the thought life of their minds and the emotions of their hearts. Choose what you will take into your life and what you will reject.

When you hear a negative comment about yourself—or about any aspect of life—dispose of it immediately. Refuse to take it into your life to think about it, dwell on it, or be influenced by it.

When you hear a positive comment about yourself—even

if it's one you have to voice to yourself in the mirror!—choose to focus on that thought.

Choose to read what builds you up as a person and makes you have more hope.

Choose to listen to messages that cause you to love yourself and others more generously and genuinely.

Choose to engage in activities that strengthen you mentally, physically, and emotionally.

And above all, make these choices on a daily basis. Daily fight your inner battle against intimidating problems, circumstances, and relationships. To move from being a grasshopper to a giant slayer in your mental perspective, you need to grow.

The best growth is consistent, slow, steady, daily growth. You can grow in this manner if you feed on the positive in your mind and heart. Take in what will cause you to grow. Refuse what will inhibit your growth.

Choose today to begin a move toward no longer being a grasshopper in your own eyes!

CHAPTER 4

Avoiding
Friendly
Fire

D uring the Gulf War, and even more recently
during investigations and hearings regarding a
downed helicopter flying on a United Nations
mission over Iraq, we have heard about the sad and serious
consequences of friendly fire.

Friendly fire is a military term used to describe the results
when aircraft, military installations, and valued personnel are
destroyed inadvertently by their own armed forces. Sometimes
the error is caused by a mechanical or technological malfunc-
tion. Very often, however, the tragedy stems from human
error. In those cases, the victims are not only the ones who
are killed by the friendly fire but, psychologically, those who
have caused the death and destruction.

Many people also acquire grasshopper mentality through
friendly fire. People nearly always learn grasshopper mentality first in the home from parents and siblings, and very often
from well-meaning and loving parents and siblings. In some
school situations, administrators and teachers reinforce this
mind-set. Finally, churches, playmates, and even television
programs can add a layer of reinforcement so that the perspective becomes deeply ingrained: *I am not worthy to fly.*
Rather, I am continually shot down.

Consider the friendly fire messages that were sent to these famous people:

- Beethoven's music teacher said, "As a composer, he is hopeless."
- Thomas Edison's teacher told him he was unable to learn.
- F. W. Woolworth's employers refused to allow him to wait on customers because he "didn't have enough sense."
- Caruso's music teacher told him that he had "no voice at all."
- Louis Pasteur was given a rating of "mediocre" in chemistry at Royal College.
- A newspaper editor fired Walt Disney from his staff because he had "no good ideas."
- Henry Ford was once evaluated as "showing no promise."

Each of these people suffered from friendly fire, but they obviously refused to allow these negative bombs to go off in their lives and destroy their desire, ambition, creativity, or willingness to keep trying.

UNINTENTIONAL FIRE STILL HURTS

Most friendly fire is not intentional. It occurs because people pulling the trigger or pushing the buttons—psychologically, emotionally, and relationally speaking—are unaware of the damage they are doing to another person. In other cases, people are simply careless with their tongues and the expression of their opinions.

Some time ago, I gave a commencement address at a college. Afterward, a man came up and introduced himself to me, saying, "I serve in a leadership role for a program called Head Start, and I have 148,000 parents who need to hear your message. I would like to come to Myrtle Beach and talk to you about what you are doing in the Power of Positive Students International Foundation."

This educator did come to visit with us, and while we were watching a videotape on emotional abuse, he suddenly turned to me and said, "Bill, I didn't realize that I have been so guilty of emotionally abusing my own children. The very idea makes me sick at my stomach, and yet, I've got to face it. I never have thought about the fact that I may have been emotionally abusing my children by the way I've been talking to them. If nothing else comes from our meeting, I have learned that I must stop talking down to and screaming at my own kids."

Several weeks after our visit, he called me and told me that upon arriving home, he told his wife and daughters what he had learned and apologized to them. One of his daughters said jokingly, "Well, the next time you yell, we're going to call 911." He said, "I told them that if they called 911, they'd better call a hearse, too. They knew I was teasing, too, but even in that remark, I recognized that I was making an idle threat—which is a form of intimidation. My wife and daughters and I discussed the importance of changing the way we talked to one another in the home, and we're working at it now every day."

Many people don't realize that a great deal of unintentional friendly fire occurs within the home or is related to a person's home life.

- Did you know that two out of every three persons in our nation's prisons come from broken homes?
- Some 1.1 million children each year are emotionally abused—primarily at home.
- Verbal and nonverbal abuse is a growing problem in spite of all the publicity and television talk shows devoted to the problem in recent years.

Many people are coming to regard our school systems as repair shops for children who come to school in a broken state. A decade ago, few teachers were trained in character building programs, were asked to teach morals or basic safety principles, or engaged in psychological pretesting of their students. The child who came to school abused physically was a rare exception. In terms of sexual abuse, the estimates are as high as one in every ten young girls in elementary school has been abused sexually, and by the time girls reach high school, the estimate climbs to one in every six.

In describing the end of the age, Jesus said to His disciples, "A man's enemies will be those of his own household" (Matt. 10:36). No doubt many children believe that day is upon them.

AN ARSENAL OF VERBAL WEAPONS

There are at least six types of statements that we make in assaulting other people verbally:

1. *Negative team building.* This occurs when we say things that make people feel they are not a part of the team or their contribution to a team effort doesn't count.

2. *Negative conditioning.* A person repeatedly plants negative thoughts into the mind of another person. Unfortunately, we can inflict this type of friendly fire upon ourselves. The fact is that most of the self-defeating put-downs we hear are self-spoken or self-thought. More than 93 percent of our self-talk tends to be negative, self-defeating, and self-limiting.

3. *Negative reinforcement.* Grasshopper mentality is also caused by people who are constantly finding fault with what others do, and who are never looking for the good that they are or that they accomplish. A person might do five things right and only one thing wrong, but the person pulling the friendly fire trigger notices only the one thing wrong.

4. *Negative climate.* The communication, conversations, and media messages that most of us encounter on a daily basis are filled with negative messages. Some have estimated that 80 percent of the messages we hear in a day are negative.

5. *Negative self-talk passed on.* When we engage in negative self-talk, others frequently hear us mumbling, and our negative attitude and words spread to the point where others

unconsciously begin mumbling negative things to themselves.

6. *Negative modeling*. People frequently model nonverbal behaviors that cause others to feel inferior or intimidated.

Every person is capable of firing verbal zingers:

"You look great. How many more pounds are you hoping to lose?"

"Why are you wasting your time shooting hoops? You're never going to be tall enough to be a basketball player."

"I hear your son finally got a job. What strings did you pull?"

> ■
> ***Humor is a good way to defuse a verbal bomb.***
> ■

"Well, I see you are doing one of the things you do best—loafing."

I heard a woman describe a childhood experience. When she was twelve years old, she was combing her hair in front of a bathroom mirror, and her mother said to her, "Don't worry, honey. If your nose gets any bigger, we can have it fixed." The woman said, "Up until that time, it had never occurred to me that anything was wrong with my nose!"

People will often preface their verbal assaults with a comment such as:

"I'm only looking out for your best interests."

"Please take this as constructive criticism."

"I hope you don't mind if I'm honest with you."

When you hear statements such as those, run for cover!

PUTTING AN END TO FRIENDLY FIRE

If you are an adult, you need to be aware that you may be the target of friendly fire. Be alert to the subtle, unconscious, and unwitting ways that those with whom you live, work, worship, and serve may be causing you to acquire grasshopper mentality.

If you are a parent, a teacher, or other person who works with children, be aware that you may be firing on those you love.

A conscious and conscientious effort is necessary to avoid causing friendly fire. Building a giant-slayer mentality in yourself and those you love requires a deliberate effort to build high self-esteem in yourself and other people at all times.

Be aware of these factors that can cause you to be more prone to verbally or nonverbally firing on your family, friends, and self:

- Overexhaustion. We frequently say things we don't mean when we are overly tired.
- Too much stress. Unresolved stress related to work, relationship difficulties, health problems, or sin in our lives can cause us to lash out at others or to ignore them. Stress can cause everything in our lives to be exaggerated—waiting in line causes us to lose our patience when we might otherwise strike up a conversation with the person in front of us, the traffic causes us to erupt in anger when we otherwise would use it as a time to listen to music or rehearse a speech, a minor mistake causes us to throw up our hands in despair when we otherwise would laugh at our foibles.

> ■ *Give people the benefit of the doubt.* ■

- Times of crisis. In crisis times—whether a crisis caused by a natural disaster, an accident, a health problem, or some other difficulty—we often speak without thinking, and those spur-of-the-moment statements may very well be a reflection of the negative circumstance or situation we are facing.

The number of people who literally lose their lives as the result of a disaster or unavoidable tragedy are a speck in the ocean compared to the vast numbers of people who on a daily basis contribute to their own self-destruction or the destruction of others psychologically and emotionally.

PUTTING UP A SHIELD OF DEFENSE

Very often we can divert incoming friendly fire by taking some simple actions.

First, choose to look behind the insult at the person. Those who fire verbal insults and negative comments are frequently hurting in some way. They often are speaking out of their hurt more than they are intending to hurt you. Don't take personally what they say.

Second, wait a little while before responding. Don't be too quick to fire back. That's the way to get a full-blown war started! However, confront an insult when both of you are calm. Never respond when you are upset at having been attacked verbally or when the other person is still attacking. Wait until you are alone with the person, and then as calmly as possible, express your feelings and your desires. Make certain that you know what you are feeling and what changes in behavior you would like to see.

Third, respond with humor whenever you can. Humor is a good way to defuse a verbal bomb. I read in *Reader's Digest* an article in which a person asked, "A new skirt? That looks like material you'd use to upholster a chair." The woman wearing the skirt replied, "Well, come sit in my lap." Insults rarely stick if you agree with your attacker in a light tone of voice.

Fourth, remember the 10 percent factor. This age-old axiom goes something like this:

- No matter what you paid for an item, somebody somewhere probably paid 10 percent less.
- About 10 percent of the time, something you lend will be returned to you damaged.
- Ten percent of the time, even your best friend may say something thoughtless and hurtful.
- At any given moment, there's probably 10 percent something wrong with your automobile.

No matter how good something may be, it probably has a 10 percent failure rate. Give people the benefit of the doubt. They may be falling into the 10 percent category.

Fifth, refuse to accept the criticism. Not everything everybody says to you is true. You must be the judge of whether the comment is factual, actual, applicable, or consequential. The questions to ask are these:

- Is what he said rooted in fact, or is it just his opinion?
- Is what she said really the case, or is it what she wishes were true?
- Is this really about me? Is the person just spouting off and venting, or is he really talking about me personally?
- Does it matter? Will my life be affected in a negative way if I don't act on this statement, respond to it, or change my behavior?

The story is told about a wise man who was attacked verbally. He turned to the person who had verbally abused him and asked, "If someone declined to accept a present given to him, to whom would the present belong?"

The person who had fired the insult said, "To the person who offered the gift."

The wise man then replied, "I agree. And I decline to accept the gift of your verbal abuse."

VERBAL VITAMINS—WORDS THAT BUILD UP!

We need to recognize that just as verbal zingers can defeat and destroy and, ultimately, create a grasshopper mentality, so too, verbal vitamins can be of a positive nature. Verbal vitamins go a long way toward building up a giant-slayer mentality:

"Atta boy!"

"Way to go!"

"Congratulations."

"Thank you."

"I appreciate you."

"I love having you around."

"You did a super job."

"I'm proud of you."

When we share these words with others, we are building them up on the inside and helping to create something positive in their lives.

We need to speak similar words to ourselves:

"I did my best, and that's all that can be expected."

"I trust God."

"I did a good job for them, even if they don't recognize it or appreciate it."

"I'm worthy."

"I'm valuable to this organization, even if the executives don't know my name."

"I am *somebody.*"

Many years ago, I read a charming story about a young man named Johnny Lingo. In the primitive culture in which Johnny Lingo lived, a young man who desired to marry a particular maiden had to bargain with her father for her. The fathers of the village demanded payment for their daughters generally in the form of cows. Two or three cows could buy an above-average wife, and four or five a very beautiful wife!

Johnny Lingo was the brightest, strongest, and most handsome young man in the village. He was fond of a young maiden named Sarita, and he set out to ask her father to give her to him as a wife. Sarita most generously could have been described as being plain. She was not truly ugly, but she was not very attractive, either. She was very shy, afraid to speak up or laugh in public. And to further deflate her value in the eyes of most of the villagers, she was a little older than most maidens at the time of marriage. Still, Johnny Lingo loved her.

■

When we value those around us, we increase their value.

■

The villagers' favorite topic of conversation at such a time was to gossip about the bargaining price of a young maiden. Some whispered that Johnny Lingo might offer two cows, three at the most. Others whispered that they thought Sarita's father might even settle for one cow since nobody else seemed interested in Sarita and Johnny Lingo was a shrewd trader.

When the time came for Johnny to meet with Sarita's father, Johnny walked boldly into the presence of Sarita's father, grasped his hand, and said, "Father of Sarita, I offer eight cows for your daughter."

Word spread through the village like wildfire. Everyone was astonished. That was the highest price ever paid for a bride in their village! The word began to be passed from house to house, "Surely, a mistake has been made. Perhaps Johnny Lingo was exaggerating. Could it be that he will actually pay eight cows?"

Johnny Lingo was as good as his word, and shortly thereafter, he herded eight cows to his future father-in-law. The wedding was held that same evening.

As the weeks and months passed, Sarita underwent a startling transformation. Her bearing became that of a queen. The sparkle in her eyes was dazzling, and she moved and spoke with striking grace and poise. People who came to the village and had never seen Sarita before began to remark that she was the most beautiful woman in the region.

Much later, someone asked Johnny Lingo why he paid such a high price for Sarita. Why offer eight cows when he could have had her as his wife for three? Did he make such a high offer just to make Sarita happy?

"Happy?" he asked. "Yes, I wanted her to be happy, but I wanted more than that. Many things can change a woman. Things that happen inside, and things that happen outside. But the most important thing that changes a woman is how she thinks about herself. Before, Sarita believed she was worth nothing. Now she knows she is worth more than any other woman in the village."

After a brief pause, Johnny Lingo concluded, "I loved Sarita and no other woman. And I wanted to marry her. But I also wanted an eight-cow wife."

When we value those around us, we increase their value.

When we value those around us, they value themselves more.

When we value those around us, our perspective about them changes.

CHAPTER 5

Wiping
the Slate
Clean

D o you remember the chalkboards you had in the classrooms of your childhood? I certainly do.

Those were the days before the white surfaces and special markers we find in many schools today. Those were the days of chalk and erasers, and at the end of the day, special chamois erasers truly wiped the black or green board clean.

Even before that type of board became popular, however, teachers and students wrote on slate. An eraser wasn't enough to remove completely the marks made during the day. Genuine slate surfaces needed to be washed clean with soap and water.

Many people need a good scrubbing to remove all traces of grasshopper mentality from their thinking. For them, grasshopper mentality is rooted not in what others say and do in their presence or in the present tense of their lives but in their memories of past humiliation, insults, personal failures, and fears.

Scientists tell us that our memories can be just as potent as our current senses. We all know that to be true to a certain extent. Just the memory of a particular moment can cause our stomachs to tense, our palms to become clammy, or our temples to throb. In other instances, good memories can give us a chuckle, bring a smile to the face, or help us relax. We all know how a certain aroma can bring back memories of special meals, even to the point that the saliva starts to build up in our mouths, or how the sound of a certain song can bring back memories of a special time and set our toes to tapping.

The person with grasshopper mentality tends to have painful memories. Not only that, but the person can't seem to leave behind the memories. Instead, they are brought back to mind again and again, each time reinforcing the pain a bit more. The memories are like old words on a slate that are never fully erased, memories that need to be washed clean from the slate so that not even a faint impression of them lingers.

In keeping with the idea of erasers, and recalling Dr. Peale's statement in chapter 1, the great motivational speaker and writer has said this about his past in his autobiography, *True Joy of Positive Living:*

> As a young man, I was anything but a positive thinker. In fact, I had a dominating inferiority complex. Learning how to shake it off and live normally was one of the greatest problems I ever had to face in life. I had some ambitious dreams and set big goals. I had boundless enthusiasm and energy. But, I was plagued by self-doubt and feelings of inadequacy. I endured the sneering message from my subconscious: "you can't do it, you haven't got what it takes."

> A professor at Ohio Wesleyan University said, "You have an inferiority complex that you've been nursing until it dominates you."

> Another teacher said, "See that eraser? A wonderful thing, an eraser. It can rub out mistakes, make the paper clean," and hurling it against the desk, he said, "Look at the bounce it's got built into it. The same thing with you, son. Wipe out that inferiority attitude, get the bounce going that almighty God built into you. Let the Lord remake you."

Dr. Peale prayed, "Can't You also change a poor, defeated boy like me, into a normal person? Please do, dear Lord."

What a good prayer for all people with grasshopper mentality to pray! The good news is that when we come to God with this prayer, He says that He will wipe the slate clean for us as far as He is concerned.

In 1 John 1:9, we find these encouraging words: "If we confess our sins, He is faithful and just to forgive us our sins and to cleanse us from all unrighteousness." It's up to us to receive His forgiveness and accept that His cleansing truly wipes out any old messages on the slate. Seeking and receiving God's forgiveness is the first step.

The second step we need to take is to forgive ourselves. That sounds easier than it is. For many people, it's not enough to say one time, "I won't let that bother me again," or "I forgive myself and I'll never think about this again."

THE FIGHT *AGAINST* NEGATIVE FEELINGS

Instead, most of us need to fight the negative idea each time it bubbles back up in memory. How do we do that? My best suggestion is to think about something else instead— and very specifically, to think about something positive.

It can be done!

- When you relive the past mistake and are inclined to say, "I shouldn't have done that," say instead, "I won't do that in the future. I'll . . . ," and then, map out a game plan you would follow if you were in a similar circumstance.

When you kick yourself mentally over a missed opportunity, instead of beating yourself up with thoughts of, *I really blew it,* say to yourself, "I'm going to be on the lookout for new opportunities every day." Ask for God's help, saying, "Lord, please help me not to miss anything You have for me."

When you are discouraged by the cutting or insulting remark somebody made about you or directly to you, rather than think, *He is right; I really am what he says,* say, "He doesn't know the full truth about me, which is that I'm not who he thinks I am at all!" Think about the many wonderful qualities that the Lord has planted in your life, about the experiences He has given you, and about how much God says He loves you.

To get rid of weeds in your garden, you have to do two things—pull out the weed, and plant a good seed in its place. If you only pull out the weed and fail to replant, the vacant soil is going to be loosened and ready for the next weed seed that happens to come floating along.

YOU CAN REFUSE TO LET
MESSAGES STICK

Teflon coating is one of the most popular inventions of our century. Cooks everywhere have praised Teflon-coated pots and pans, which they can wipe clean.

The person who refuses to hang on to grasshopper mentality and who wants to develop giant-slaying thinking in its place needs to Teflon coat the mind to negative ideas and hurtful remarks.

It can be done! Some of the most famous people in history apparently have had the ability to let certain ideas roll right off their minds, like unwanted food particles on Teflon-coated pans.

Isaac Newton's work in elementary school was considered to be poor. He didn't let that evaluation stop him.

Einstein didn't talk until he was four years old, and he didn't read until the age of seven. Apparently, he didn't have any sense of failure about that.

Louisa May Alcott was told by an editor that her writings would never appeal to the public. She kept writing anyway, producing some of the most popular books of all time.

Leo Tolstoy flunked out of college. He didn't internalize that to the point where it kept him from a phenomenal career.

Admiral Richard Byrd was deemed "unfit for service." That

evaluation didn't stop him from eventually flying over both of the earth's poles.

Winston Churchill failed the sixth grade, and Fred Waring once failed to get into his high school chorus. Neither man let the experience become a setback or a psychological stumbling block.

You may not go on to world renown or genius-level contributions, but then again, you just may. Ultimately, you and the Lord are the only two people who can recognize, appreciate, value, and begin to realize your full potential as a person. But the Lord can't turn you into somebody you don't believe you can be.

A man named Gideon learned that lesson in a dramatic way.

FROM A SCARED NOBODY TO A MIGHTY MAN OF VALOR

One day Gideon was threshing wheat in a winepress—a rather wimpy action to take in an effort to hide grain from taxation by the ruling Midianites. The Angel of the Lord appeared to Gideon and said, "The LORD is with you, you mighty man of valor!"

Up to that point, Gideon had displayed no might or valor at all. He was secretly threshing wheat with one eye over his shoulder, running scared in all areas of his life. The Lord, however, knew Gideon's potential for valor, and He called to him with words of encouragement.

Gideon responded, "If the LORD is with us, why then has all this happened to us?" Gideon totally failed to see how the Lord had provided for him, for his family, or for his people. He didn't even acknowledge what the Lord had said about him. He focused only on the negative circumstances he saw all around him. He exhibited grasshopper thinking at its worst!

The Angel of the Lord didn't give up. He turned to Gideon

and said, "Go in this might of yours, and you shall save Israel from the hand of the Midianites. Have I not sent you?"

Although Gideon seemingly ignored what the Lord had said about him, the Angel refused to fall into the trap of Gideon's negative thinking. He again pointed to Gideon's might and the mission God had for his life.

Gideon replied in classic grasshopper-mentality fashion, "O my Lord, how can I save Israel? Indeed my clan is the weakest in Manasseh, and I am the least in my father's house." Gideon was saying, in other words, "I'm a nobody with nothing."

Thank God that He doesn't give up on us! Two times Gideon spoke negatively to the messenger of God, and yet the Angel generously and patiently spoke to Gideon again, "Surely I will be with you, and you shall defeat the Midianites as one man."

Two popular expressions we hear today are, "Work with me on this," and "Go with me on this." The meaning is that the person speaking wants the other person to go along with his thinking for a little bit to see whether the idea might take hold. That's what the Angel was doing with Gideon. You can almost hear him say, "Just work with me a little on this, Gideon. Go with me on this idea, and let's see what happens."

Gideon began to respond, ever so slightly: "If now I have found favor in Your sight, then show me a sign that it is You who talk with me. Do not depart from here, I pray, until I come to You and bring out my offering and set it before You."

The closed door of Gideon's mind was opened a tiny bit. The Lord was patient. He said, "I will wait until you come back."

The wait was quite a long one, and all the while, you can almost sense that Gideon must have been hoping the messenger would go away. Gideon took time to kill, skin, and cook a young goat, bake bread from scratch, and bring out a full meal, including soup, to the waiting Angel.

The Angel directed Gideon to put the meat and bread on a nearby rock, and to pour the broth over them. Then the

Angel took his staff and touched the meat and bread, and fire rose up out of the rock and completely consumed the meat and bread. Immediately, the Angel disappeared.

Given such a dramatic demonstration of the Angel's power, Gideon finally caught on! He cried out, "Alas, O Lord GOD!" But very quickly, grasshopper mentality overwhelmed him once again: "I have seen the Angel of the LORD face to face." To the Israelites, that was a death sentence since they believed that nobody could look upon God and live; His power and majesty were too great.

The Lord said to Gideon directly, "Peace be with you; do not fear, you shall not die." And Gideon responded by building an altar to God.

Something must have happened to Gideon while he was making that altar. He must have thought to himself, *Maybe what the Lord has said about me is true. Maybe, just maybe, I should believe the Lord and accept His word rather than believe my circumstances and what I think about myself.*

The next time the Lord spoke to Gideon, which happened to be during the night of that very same day, Gideon responded with a completely different attitude. He didn't hesitate, didn't ask questions, didn't make any derogatory remarks about himself, and didn't question the Lord's ability or directives, even though they were fairly awesome.

The Lord told Gideon to cut down the altar to Baal that was on his father's property and also to cut down the sacred image beside it. In its place, he was to build another altar and sacrifice a bull using the wood from the cut-down image. For a son to take such action against something his enemies had built and his father had protected was an outrageous and rebellious act. Still, Gideon was beginning to get an inkling of just what God thought of him, and he was beginning to adopt a mind-set that he just might be a "mighty man of valor."

The next night, Gideon took ten of the household servants and cut down the altar of Baal and the sacred image, and they sacrificed a bull on the second altar they built.

His actions brought on a major confrontation with the people in his town and, eventually, the Midianites and Amalekites, who crossed over and encamped in the Valley of Jezreel. The old Gideon—the one beset with grasshopper mentality—would no doubt have run away and hidden from the advancing trouble. But not the new Gideon, the one who had adopted a giant-slaying "mighty man of valor" perspective about himself. The Spirit of the Lord came upon Gideon, and he blew a trumpet, which was a direct challenge for war. He sent messengers throughout the land to call the people to battle against their enemies. Men from all the surrounding tribes began to arrive on the scene.

Only the Lord sees your full potential.

And even so, a bit of grasshopper mentality came creeping back into Gideon. He went again to God and said, "If You will save Israel by my hand as You have said . . ."

"If" statements are very often a sign of grasshopper mentality:

"If You are who You say You are . . ."

"If I am who You say I am . . ."

"If it comes to pass as You have said it will . . ."

"If I am to believe . . ."

Gideon laid out two tests of the Lord, and when those two tests came back "positive," Gideon finally had giant-slaying thinking firmly embedded inside him. (See Judg. 6:12–40.)

WANTED: AN ARMY OF GIANT SLAYERS

The Lord knew that not everybody who answered Gideon's call had giant-slaying thinking. The Lord said to Gideon, "Proclaim in the hearing of the people, saying, 'Whoever is fearful and afraid, let him turn and depart at once.'" Of the thirty-two thousand people who had gathered, twenty-two thousand left. Two out of three people who had come to the spring of Harod to fight with Gideon turned away at the first opportunity. Two out of three had grasshopper mentality, even though they had volunteered for war. (How many tens of thousands of people with grasshopper mentality had stayed at home?)

Even with only ten thousand left, not all had giant-slaying belief. The Lord told Gideon to take them to the spring and drink. Those who kneeled to drink the water still had grasshopper mentality—they did not stay alert even when drinking. Of the ten thousand, nine thousand seven hundred had a little grasshopper mentality, and they were sent home. Only three hundred lapped the water cautiously, and they were the ones Gideon was told to keep for the battle ahead.

Second chances will come your way as you trust God.

Three hundred out of thirty-two thousand volunteers! Can it be that giant-slaying mentality is just that rare today?

From my experience and observation in traveling across our nation and to many other lands, it is. The fact, however, is that all can have giant-slaying thinking. No person needs to have grasshopper mentality. We are challenged to believe about ourselves what God alone thinks about us, and not what others say to us or about us or even what we think about ourselves.

Only the Lord sees your full potential. He is waiting for you to respond, "Okay, Lord, I'll go with You on this. I choose to believe about myself what You believe about me."

A MIGHTY VICTORY FOR THE 1 PERCENT

The Lord had a strange battle plan for Gideon. Gideon and his three hundred men were to take rams' horns as trumpets and clay pitchers with torches in them. Upon a signal, the men were to blow their trumpets, and then they were to break their pitchers, revealing the torches, and shout.

Gideon didn't even question whether the plan would work. God had given a dream to a man about a loaf of bread tumbling down into the Midianite camp and toppling a tent.

His companion thought it was a sign from the Lord that Gideon would prevail. Gideon heard them talking about the dream and its interpretation, and he in turn went to all those remaining and said, "Arise, for the LORD has delivered the camp of Midian into your hand." By that time, Gideon was displaying solid giant-slaying confidence.

Note something very important, however. Gideon hadn't put his trust in himself or in the brilliance of the battle plan given to him. He didn't trust the soldiers and their commitment. He said, "The LORD has delivered the camp of Midian into your hand." Gideon had giant-slaying confidence *because he placed his confidence in the Lord*. He fully believed God and what God said about the matter, and because of that, he fully anticipated victory.

And victory was what Gideon and his band of three hundred men experienced. When the trumpets were blown, the Midianite soldiers arose and heard clay pots breaking, saw torches shining, and heard shouts from the hills all around them. They fell into such a panic they started killing one another. Many fled in fear. And eventually, they were completely driven from the land. (See Judg. 7.)

Consider for just a moment what would have happened if Gideon stubbornly had retained his old grasshopper mentality.

How many more years would Israel have suffered under the Midianites?

Who would have earned Gideon's place in God's Word as an example of how God can deliver His people if they are only willing to obey Him and believe about themselves what He believes about them?

How might the life of Gideon have been different?

When we start to believe what God believes about us—wiping the slate clean of our past negative ideas and feelings—God puts us into position to experience a second chance, another opportunity, a turnaround moment. He puts us into a sequence of experiences and events that result in victory for ourselves and for all of God's people.

Along the way, we must seize each opportunity He gives us. We must follow through on each good thing and good idea He commands us to do.

SEIZING THE SECOND CHANCE

Second chances will come your way as you trust God. Sometimes you may have a part in engineering them. Sometimes they may seem to come to you in a totally unexpected way and at an unexpected time. In whatever way a second-chance opportunity presents itself, seize it!

The great football coach at Notre Dame, Lou Holtz, knows about second chances and writes about them in *Grit, Guts and Genius* (Houghton, Mifflin Co., 1990). In 1966, when Holtz was only twenty-eight years old, he was hired as an assistant coach to Marvin Bass at the University of South Carolina. Holtz's wife, Beth, was eight months pregnant at the time, and Holtz spent virtually every penny he had to make a down payment on a house. One month after Holtz was hired, Bass quit his job to go to the Canadian Football League, and Lou Holtz was left unemployed and struggling.

Then his wife bought him *The Magic of Thinking Big* by David Schwartz. Holtz hadn't read much before that. In fact, he wasn't motivated to do much of anything. He has said about himself, "There are so many people, and I was one of them, who don't do anything special with their lives." At the lowest point of his life, however, he was desperate.

The book by Schwartz suggested that a reader write down all the goals he wanted to achieve by the time he died. Holtz gave it a try. He came up with 107 goals. They included have dinner at the White House, see the pope, be on Johnny Carson's show, jump out of an airplane, win a national championship, and be coach of the year. He recalls that the more he wrote, the more excited he became about his life. Holtz had tapped into his dreams and, along with them, the possibility of a second chance. He has said about that experience, "My whole life changed."

Armed with this new attitude, Holtz began to study the Bible and also the lives of great coaches. He began to form the philosophy that he, in turn, has taught every team he has coached.

Not only did Lou Holtz have a second-chance, turnaround experience in his life, but he began to lead team after team through turnaround experiences. Before coaching at Notre Dame, Holtz coached at four other colleges: William and Mary, North Carolina State, the University of Arkansas, and the University of Minnesota. In each case, he inherited a losing team and wound up taking the team to a bowl game in his second year at the school.

While at Arkansas, his team faced Oklahoma in the 1978 Orange Bowl. Oklahoma was favored by 23 points, and the Arkansas players knew it. They were downcast as a team, preparing to lose. Holtz called a team meeting and asked each athlete to stand and say why he thought Arkansas could win. As the players stood, one by one, and pointed out the team's many pluses, Holtz recalls that "the whole attitude changed." The players had an unbelievably good practice the next day, and people later told Holtz that they knew Arkansas would win the Orange Bowl simply by looking at the faces of the players as they ran out of the locker room onto the field. Arkansas beat Oklahoma 31–6.

Holtz also called a team meeting after Notre Dame lost the Cotton Bowl to Texas A&M in 1987. He gave what the players came to call "The Perfection Speech." Holtz presented to his players the vision he had for their lives—how they would be perfect in the classroom, practice the best, and be perfect men in their overall lives. He then asked all those in the room who wanted to win the national championship in 1988 to stand up. Everybody in the room stood. That set the turnaround, second-chance tone for Notre Dame, which did indeed win the 1988 college football championship.

Several things about Lou Holtz stand out to me.

First, he factors God into his life. Lou Holtz doesn't attempt to realize his dreams or seize his second chances without turning to his Bible and to the Lord.

Second, even in the face of a defeat, he sets a bigger goal—not only for himself but for his teams.

Third, he pursues his goals with effort and persistence. Notre Dame didn't get to the top by desire alone. Holtz adds to his inspirational and excellent game-day coaching the basics: an emphasis on the fundamentals, twice-a-day practices, and 6:00 A.M. conditioning workouts.

Fourth, he wants his players to have character, even more than he wants them to wear championship rings. Holtz teaches his teams these three basic rules: (1) do what's right, (2) do your very best, and (3) treat others like you'd like to be treated. They sound like simple ideas, and they are, but they are at the very core of Holtz's winning philosophy. They are the positive ideas that Holtz attempts to implant into athletes to make them true giant-slaying champions both on and off the field.

In an era when many sports figures have become tainted for lack of character, I'm grateful for men such as Lou Holtz and Bobby Bowden at Florida State, who are active in the Fellowship of Christian Athletes, Dean Smith at North Carolina, Joe Paterno at Penn State, and Bill McCartney, founder of the Promise Keepers, who are strong, outstanding men and Christian leaders.

They are giant slayers in themselves, and they are teaching other men how to be giant slayers, too.

WIPING THE SLATE CLEAN

Another football standout exemplifies having been given a second chance. The man is Coach Gene Stallings.

When the president of the University of Alabama, Dr. Roger Sayers, and the athletic director, "Hootie" Ingram, began looking for a head coach to replace Billy Curry, who had resigned as coach of Alabama to take a position at Kentucky, the name Gene Stallings was put in the hopper.

Even though Stallings had played for the legendary Coach Paul "Bear" Bryant at Texas A&M, there were those who thought that at age fifty-five he was too old for the job. Others questioned his records as a coach at Texas A&M and with the Phoenix Cardinals, both of which were losing records. Still, the University of Alabama selection committee hired him. In speaking to the press after being hired, Stallings thanked the university's president and selection committee and said of his own life and coaching as a career that he was "wiping the slate clean."

Three years later, when the votes were tallied, Alabama was unanimously voted the 1992 NCAA football championship team. Alabama had won thirteen games that season and lost none. The team's winning streak had been extended to twenty-three games.

■ *Start each day with a clean slate.*

■

Coach Stallings said, "I've thought a lot about Hootie and Dr. Sayers taking a chance on me. I didn't have the best record in the world. I had a losing record at the time as a former head coach at Texas A&M (45–51–1) and the Cardinals (23–34–1). I don't know the right words to explain how much I appreciate them for taking a chance on me. I've told them that, too. I am a lucky man. Only in America can you be fired twice and become Coach of the Year."

A humble Coach Stallings celebrated in the locker room following his team's victory over the University of Miami in the Sugar Bowl: Alabama 34, Miami 13. The win had assured Alabama of the national title, and Stallings knew what that meant not only for his team but for him as a coach. One elated fan in the dressing room was none other than Coach Stallings's son, Johnny. He greeted his dad with a hug and exclaimed, "Great job, Pop! You did okay, Pop!" Coach Stallings embraced his son, smiled, and then placed a cap on Johnny's head—a cap printed with the words "NCAA National Champions 1992." Then he said to Johnny, "We are national champions, partner . . . the national champions, son—that's big."

I had the privilege of sitting down to talk with Coach Stallings in his office in March 1993. He had just finished spring practice, and his team was scheduled to visit the president of the United States the following day. High school coaches, parents, and prospective players were all waiting in his outer office to see him. Still, he gave unselfishly of his time to discuss a project with me.

As I drove back to South Carolina after our meeting, I thought about how many lives Gene Stallings had touched in a positive way during the previous three years he had been at the university—all of which had been made possible because university officials were willing to give him a second chance, and he was willing to wipe the slate clean in his life and take on a new job with a fresh perspective, renewed energy, and a drive toward excellence. He and the people who had hired him refused to allow the circumstances or records of the past to keep him from the opportunity to take the Crimson Tide back to the top.

Are you willing to wipe the slate clean in your life? Is someone giving you a second chance, willing to give you the opportunity to start over, but you are clutching to doubts and memories that keep you rooted in past failure? If so, you need to wipe your slate clean.

STARTING EACH DAY NEW

Some people think they must wait for a special time or date to start over—perhaps January 1, their birthday, Rosh Hashanah, the Chinese new year, or the anniversary of their marriage.

In actuality, any day can be the day of a new beginning, including today. Ultimately, *every day* can be a day to start over.

The words in 2 Corinthians 5:17 hold out great promise for a clean slate: "Therefore, if anyone is in Christ, he is a new creation; old things have passed away; behold, all things have beome new."

I've found that the best way to live with joy in my heart,

a bounce in my step, and giant-slaying thinking as my perspective on life is to start each day with a clean slate.

- End each day by confessing your sins to God and accepting His forgiveness into your life.
- Greet the Lord each morning with a request that He guide and guard your steps.
- Expect something good to happen to you all the day through.

Embrace the idea that you have a clean slate for the day that lies ahead—that you are a "new creation" and that you are open to new possibilities and opportunities. Even as you are working for God all through the day, no matter what your chosen profession or responsibilities, so long as God is working in you.

And when fresh, exciting, positive, second-chance and new-chance opportunities present themselves, grab hold of them with both hands and don't let go.

CHAPTER 6

Paying
Up Front

As a young married man, I had this philosophy about spending: if we couldn't pay cash for something, we didn't buy it.

At the time, I was working for U.S. Steel, and my wife was working as a secretary. After we got paid and paid our bills, we usually went furniture shopping. Sometimes we had enough money to go at the end of a two-week period. Sometimes we needed to wait until the end of the month, depending on our bills and the cost of what we wanted to purchase. The result was that for several years, we had rooms in our apartment, and later in our house, that didn't have any furniture in them.

We had the same approach to buying cars. We saved for several years to buy a new Chevrolet Impala. We drove it proudly and kept it spotless. After all, it was ours. We had purchased it and remained debt free.

Shortly after that, I enrolled in college at Birmingham Southern, and one day, unexpectedly, my uncle came to the campus apartments where we lived. My uncle was a used car salesman, and he wanted to show me a beautiful Buick. He informed me that it was a steal, and he wanted me to have first crack at the car. The deal was that he would take my

Chevy in on trade, and I would have to pay only an additional $1,500 for the Buick. He did a real sales job on me, and I signed the papers and drove the Buick home.

You would think that I would be happy at the prospect of driving home a new car. Quite the opposite. I was miserable. Within a matter of hours, I realized that I had gone against everything I believed in, and that I had greatly mixed emotions about being $1,500 in debt. I had gone with the flow of someone else's opinion and purchased a car that was too expensive for us.

Never having purchased anything before on credit, I had not counted on the load that a monthly payment can be. I certainly hadn't realized that the payment I made each month for the car did not necessarily reduce my principal debt. After a year of making car payments, the balance on the car was not much lower than it had been the day I first purchased the car.

Two years passed. The debt on that car continued to haunt me, even after I finished college and began coaching and teaching. I felt like a slave to the finance company.

One afternoon the father of one of my players came to talk to me after practice. He was a used car salesman. I asked him what kind of cars he sold. He said primarily Chevrolets and Fords. He asked me, "Coach, what are you driving?" I told him a Buick.

Then I asked him if he had a paid-for car he would swap for the Buick and its debt.

He went with me to take a look at my car in the parking lot, and then he said, "I'm driving a 1954 blue Ford. It is parked over by the gym. Take a look at it and see if you like it." I did, and I told him so.

He said, "Well, I'm willing to trade you my car for your car."

I asked him, "You'll take over the payments on the Buick and pay off the debt against it?"

He agreed. "It's a deal," I said. We walked directly into my office and wrote out a sales contract. Before I went home from practice that night, we had a "done deal." In fact, we traded keys, and I drove home in the 1954 Ford.

My wife could hardly believe that I had traded away our nearly new Buick for an old Ford. I responded to her, "It may be an old Ford, but it's a no-debt Ford. I'm free of debt. And never again am I going to get into that trap."

My colleagues at the school couldn't believe I had traded cars, but I never regretted that decision for a moment. I was as happy about my old 1954 Ford as I could be.

In purchasing that new Buick, I had created a giant for myself where no giant had existed.

ARE YOU CREATING A GIANT THAT WASN'T THERE BEFORE?

Many people seem to create giants for themselves. Debt is certainly one such giant.

Debt, however, is a giant that need not have been faced by most of the people who are now threatened by it. Debt occurs in most instances when we refuse to pay the price up front. Rather, we opt for credit, a pledge against our future ability to pay.

One Friday evening my wife, older son Bill, and I were having dinner at a restaurant in Auckland, New Zealand. Jo was our waitress. She was exceptionally polite and skilled as a waitress so we tipped her well. The next day we took a boat trip out to the islands. We left our boat and took a hike up a mountain where we were served a picnic lunch. To our surprise, the person serving us lunch spoke to us and called our names. It was Jo.

She said she recalled our names because we had been gracious to her.

I said, "Jo, with your skills and politeness, you must be making a ton of money as a waitress."

She replied, "Dr. Mitchell, I am a college student. I have a goal of graduating from Auckland College. I want to be a teacher. The only way I can achieve my goal is to pay the price up front and to work hard. The rewards will be worth the price I pay now."

We boarded the boat headed for Pai Hai, and the captain commented that we all should "think positively" so the sun would come out for our return trip. Sure enough, the sun made its appearance. I like to think it was partly for Jo's sake. Jo is a young woman willing to pay up front for what she wants. Part of the joy she will experience when she graduates from college will be knowing that she has graduated debt free. She will have avoided creating a giant of debt.

THE GIANTS WE CREATE IN FORGING RELATIONSHIPS

Other people seem to get themselves into one sticky situation after another, making deals with people they shouldn't go into business with, forging relationships that they sense are unhealthy from the outset, accepting employment with people they don't like, or agreeing to provide a service or manufacture a product they don't use or can't fully endorse. Eventually, these messy dealings become giants in their lives.

I have faced such a giant. Even though my grandmother taught me that a person's good name is better than silver or gold—advice that King Solomon offered in the book of Proverbs—I overlooked that wisdom. At the age of fifty-five, I entered into a real estate venture with some people who did not believe that a person should individually bear the weight of debt.

The venture was a $2 million project, and the pro forma showed that there would be more than $3 million in profit. I saw an opportunity to make several hundred thousand dollars, and an evaluation of the profit became more important to me than an evaluation of the character of my partners.

Unfortunately, the deal went sour. The result was a tremendous loss of financial resources and time for my wife and me.

I had grown up with the value that each person pays his fair share. I had taught this to my students in my role as a teacher. But I found that isn't necessarily true in the business world. I heard expressions that I had never heard before such as, "Well, that's just business. No hard feelings."

Practice works.

Because I had been careless about the associations I made, I created a giant for myself and my family. We went through four years of legal hassles that cost us thousands of dollars in legal fees.

When I look back over those years, my advice to my sons and grandchildren would be, "Make sure you aren't careless in selecting your business associates. There are many people in the world who work full-time in trying to get what you have spent your lifetime earning. Don't be careless in your social relationships, either. You may be creating a giant for yourself and your family that wouldn't exist otherwise."

Choosing a relationship is an important choice. In many ways, you become who your friends are and what your friends advise you to be and do. The matter is compounded when people aren't honest in representing themselves. Jesus taught, "Beware of false prophets, who come to you in sheep's clothing, but inwardly they are ravenous wolves" (Matt. 7:15).

How can we tell the true character of a person?

Jesus also provided the answer: "You will know them by their fruits. Do men gather grapes from thornbushes or figs from thistles? Even so, every good tree bears good fruit, but a bad tree bears bad fruit. . . . By their fruits you will know them" (Matt. 7:16–20).

To avoid creating a giant for yourself in your choice of associates and friends,

- take a look at the person's track record. How has she treated people in the past? What do others you trust say about her or know about her? What insights can you gain from her family members?
- give yourself time to get acquainted with the person. Don't make hasty judgments. Spend time together doing

things that aren't necessarily related to the project or the particular venture you are pursuing.

- talk about value issues with the person. What is really important to the person? What values do you see displayed? Do the person's stated values match up with his actions in your presence?
- watch how the person treats others who are less fortunate or who aren't in a position to do something in return for the person's kindness or help. The way "big people" treat "little people" tells a lot about their character.

In getting to know a person in advance of entering into a deal, business contract, or social obligation, you in essence are paying up front. You are finding out as much as you can about the person—making the person, rather than the venture or project, your emphasis.

GIANTS LOOM WHEN WE DON'T DO OUR HOMEWORK

Giants arise when we enter into situations that go against our values. They arise when we enter into relationships that aren't right. They also arise when we fail to do our homework or prepare ourselves for the tasks and challenges that lie ahead.

Moses didn't seek to enter Canaan unaware of the terrain or the nature of the people about to be conquered. The Lord told Moses, "Send men to spy out the land of Canaan, which I am giving to the children of Israel" (Num. 13:1).

Preparation is God's idea. We are to prepare ourselves as much as we can in advance. We are to do what we know to do and then trust God to do the rest.

Again, consider for a moment what Moses said to the spies as he sent them out:

Go up this way into the South, and go up to the mountains, and see what the land is like: whether the people who dwell in it are strong or weak, few or many; whether the land they dwell in is good or bad; whether the cities they inhabit are like camps or strongholds; whether the land is rich or poor; and whether there are forests there or not. Be of good courage. And bring some of the fruit of the land (Num. 13:17–20).

Moses was giving instructions aimed at conquest. He was looking for information that could give him insight into how the people were to be prepared to enter the land and take it. Moses did not say, "Go and see what you think about our ability to take this land." His instructions were aimed at getting information about *how* the conquest might be accomplished.

As you face various situations, ask yourself questions such as these:

- Who is involved? Few projects are done in a vacuum. Few tasks are done by oneself.
- What are the strengths and weaknesses of these people? Every project that involves others needs to make best use of each person's talent.
- What are the resources available? Every task or project takes a certain amount of time, energy, goods, and money.
- What are the obstacles we might face? Every project has certain things that must be overcome, defused, or circumvented.

Go into the decision-making process asking, How can we do it? rather than, Can we do it?

We may not be able to anticipate every problem associated with an opportunity, and I certainly am not advocating that we wait for opportunities that have no potential problems inherent in them. Such opportunities probably don't exist. I am saying that if we rush headlong into any task or project without proper evaluation and preparation—whether it is the

planning of a community fair, a fund-raising event, a development project, a college course, a particular exam, or the
organizing of a car pool—we have the potential for creating
a giant for ourselves to slay.

THE GREAT BENEFIT OF
PRACTICE GAMES

One of the foremost ways we prepare for success is through
practice. Coaches know this and put their teams through
numerous practice games and scrimmages before the season
begins. In professional sports, preseason games and exhibi-
tion games permit players to practice before the run for the
championship. Individual sportsmen are routinely given practice throws and practice serves, or trial runs.

Professional golfer Lee Trevino once said, "As long as
there's daylight, there's a golf ball to be hit." Trevino credits
practice, practice, and more practice for his transformation
into a world-class golfer or, as he says, his rise from being
lucky to talented.

The principle of practice carries over into all areas of life.
Those who speak publicly or perform on stage have found
that rehearsals help them prepare for performance.

My experiences in earning a doctoral degree
reinforced for me the value of practice. At the
time I reentered graduate school, I was the principal at one of the most prestigious schools in
Huntsville. All of the well-known scientists associated with the Space Center had their children in the school, as did most of the leaders in
town. We had just moved into a new home. I
loved my job. I liked Huntsville. But when I had the opportunity to go to the University of Alabama, I chose to give up
my career for a couple of years to get a degree that I hoped
would propel me forward to even greater opportunities.

I discovered in the process of going back to school that I
had to take an entrance exam. It loomed as a major obstacle.

*Some giants
aren't real
at all.*

I thought, *What if I don't pass? I've already given up this very nice job. What if I'm not accepted?* I passed, but I realized in looking back that even with successes under my belt, a grasshopper mentality dies hard. I was still trying to outrun the possibility of failure.

The fear I experienced about the entrance exam compelled me to take action so I wouldn't feel that same fear going into the comprehensive exams at the end of the program. I put into practice the principle of practice.

Whenever I had two or three hours free, I'd go to a professor and ask him or her to write out a question that would be the type I might expect on the comprehensive exam. I'd sit there in the general office area, giving myself a time frame to analyze the question, sort out my ideas, and write out an answer. The professors were generally quite willing to read my answers and discuss them with me. None of the other students could believe that I would take the time to do this. A few of them ridiculed me for my effort. Others accused me of tunnel vision. That may have been true, but it was the only way I knew to tackle the challenge and give it my best effort.

We can cut our losses. As it turned out, some of those who ridiculed me bombed the test and had to take another year of studies. Others had great anxiety going into the comprehensive exam stage. Since I had already put myself into that position many times before, I had no fear going into the exams. I sailed right through them. And I was one of the top graduates in the class. I say that not to brag but to state what can happen when a person develops giant-slaying thinking in place of grasshopper mentality. The kid who barely made it through high school and was given no hope of college earned a doctorate.

And not only that, but I was offered a position at the university that granted me my doctorate. One day I was a graduate student; the next I was a teacher of graduate students! My former professors, whom I had always respectfully called by their official titles and last names, suddenly were asking me to call them by their first names. I had prepared and practiced for that moment, but even so, it was a great thrill.

From that position at the University of Alabama, I was offered a superintendency of a school district.

Practice works. It destroys giants before they are fully created.

GIANTS OF OUR OWN IMAGINATIONS

Some giants aren't real at all. They are simply of our own imaginations.

Because of his sin, unrepentant heart, and unwillingness to obey God in all things, King Saul fell from favor with God. The Spirit of the Lord departed from Saul, and "a distressing spirit" troubled him. Saul's servants suggested that he seek out a person who could skillfully play the harp so that it soothed Saul's spirit. Saul said, "Provide me now a man who can play well, and bring him to me."

One of Saul's servants had heard a son of Jesse the Bethlehemite play the harp. He knew the harpist to be a mighty man of valor, a man of war, prudent in speech, a handsome person, and someone who had the Spirit of the Lord. That man was David.

And so it was that David came to Saul's court and became not only his chief musician, but his armorbearer. We are told that Saul loved David greatly.

The day came, however, when Saul's love turned to jealous hatred. David defeated Goliath and also killed a hundred other Philistines in winning the hand of Saul's daughter, Michal. Saul saw his daughter in love with David, the people of the land praising David for his victories, and the enemies of Israel fearful of David. He saw his own son, Jonathan, become more loyal to David than to himself. Most of all, Saul recognized that the Spirit of the Lord was no longer with him but was with David. Jealousy grew in his heart. And Saul sought to murder David. (See 1 Sam. 16:14–23; 18.)

David, the beloved giant slayer, had become to Saul a giant to be killed.

What had changed in David? Not a thing. He was the same David, loyal to the king and refusing to speak ill of him. David was no threat to Saul—except in Saul's mind.

Jealousy can cause us to create giants where they do not exist. These giants are among the most insidious of all because we rarely are able to back away from the person and the situation far enough to recognize the source of our own hatred, or to see the person with objective eyes.

If someone says to you, "You aren't judging that person fairly," or "You seem to be so irritated by everything that person does," take note. Are you harboring jealousy?

If you hate someone, even though he has never done anything intentional to hurt you, ask yourself, Am I really jealous of this person? Is my hatred rooted in jealousy?

Jealousy can create a giant in the imagination where none existed.

This can also happen when it comes to a person we deeply admire or like but don't know. We can turn her into a "good giant." Nevertheless, the person becomes someone we don't know how to approach, are afraid to talk to, and don't feel comfortable around in an up-close-and-personal way. We make the person into a giant, even though she might prefer to be a friend.

How can we remove these giants from our thought lives? By getting to know the person. Find out what makes the person tick—where he hurts, what causes him to rejoice. Rather than avoid the person, try to get to know him. You'll discover this made-up giant is a human being with many of the same challenges, disappointments, fears, and problems that you have. You'll probably find that you have far more in common with the person than you ever thought possible.

WE CAN SLAY THE GIANTS WE CREATE

When we create giants by doing things that go against our values and beliefs, we can ask God's forgiveness, we can return to our values, and nearly always, we can take action to reverse the bad decision or action.

When we create giants for ourselves by entering into relationships blindly, we can end destructive relationships peaceably and without malice, and make a decision to be more cautious about our relationships in the future.

When we create giants by failing to prepare ourselves adequately, we can cut our losses as soon as we recognize what we have done, and we can prepare ourselves for the next step we need to take.

Discipline requires daily diligence.

When we create giants in our own imaginations, we can ask God to cleanse the thoughts of our hearts by His Spirit, and renew a right spirit in us toward the person we have misjudged, hated, or feared.

Most of all, we can avoid these made-up, self-created giants if we will maintain our values, keep our priorities in line, and develop the self-discipline to live and act the way we claim to believe.

Maintaining Values

One of the best ways I know to maintain the values I hold to be true is to remind myself of what I believe on a daily basis. The book of values is the Bible, and especially the teachings of Jesus and the book of Proverbs. Immerse yourself in what the Bible says we are to believe and do.

Keeping Priorities in Line

Jesus taught that if we place our first emphasis on the kingdom of the Lord and on how to live in right standing with God, all of our other priorities will fall into line. In other words, if we stay in right relationship with God, we have a much better chance of staying in right relationship with other people. How do we keep that relationship right with the Lord? By talking to Him on a regular basis. If we discuss every decision, problem, action, and potential solution with the Lord in advance of pursuing it, and ask for the Lord to give us wisdom, we make much better choices.

Staying Disciplined

All discipline is ultimately self-discipline. You have to want to live a disciplined life. Find friends and mentors with whom you can talk over your desire to live a disciplined life, and put yourself into a relationship with them so that you are accountable to them for the way you live.

Ask their advice. Weigh what they say against God's Word to make sure their advice is good. Talk to the Lord about what they say to you, and listen for that "nudge" in your spirit that compels you to accept or reject what they say. If you have questions or concerns, raise them. If you come to the conclusion that their advice to you is sound, ask them for their help and encouragement as you try to do what they have advised you to do.

Discipline requires daily diligence. It doesn't happen overnight, and you can destroy years of disciplined behavior in a matter of minutes, hours, days, or weeks. The apostle Paul said we are always to be on the alert for the Enemy who comes to try to trip us up and tempt us so that we fall away from the disciplined way of life we know is right.

A GIANT STEP FORWARD IN GIANT AVOIDANCE

If we stick to our values, keep our priorities right, and maintain a disciplined life in Christ, very few giants will arise of our own making. That doesn't mean we won't face other giants. But they won't be ones that we created. In the long run, the giants we don't create are much easier for us to face and defeat than those we self-create.

CHAPTER 7

A Willingness
to Bear
Scars

F ew of us are ever able to enter a battle and emerge victorious without getting wounded in some way. The wound may not be severe, or even visible for that matter, but being wounded is nearly always a part of winning.

To face a giant—and expect to defeat it—is to be willing to bear scars. The wounds and scars we bear may result from our

- putting our reputation on the line.
- being willing to do something that makes us very nervous.
- facing the possibility of embarrassment.
- risking something that is valuable or important to us for the sake of something even more valuable or important.
- doing without or doing with less in anticipation of doing more, earning more, receiving more, or accomplishing more.
- taking one step backward in order to go two steps forward.
- listening to ridicule.

- being the brunt of gossip by little-minded people who have no understanding of the big picture.
- maintaining silence in the face of unfair criticism or mean-spirited insults.

Real victories have a price. We must be willing to pay it.

SAYING YES IN SPITE OF THE BATTLE

Jacob feared going home to face his giant. Nevertheless, he went home. The giant was his brother, Esau. And in many ways, Jacob had created this giant through his own actions. He had caught Esau in a weak moment, physically, and had tricked Esau into trading his birthright for a meal of bread and lentil stew. Just prior to the death of Isaac, their father, Jacob had masqueraded as Esau and had received Isaac's blessing. Esau was furious when he discovered what happened; he intended to kill Jacob after Isaac died and the days of mourning for him had passed.

The young men's mother, Rebekah, realized the extent of Esau's anger and hatred, and before Isaac died, she asked him to send Jacob to her brother Laban, who lived many miles away. The reason Rebekah gave to Isaac was that her life would be miserable if Jacob took a wife from Canaan, as Esau had done. Isaac did as Rebekah requested, and Jacob left immediately.

The hatred in Esau's heart seemed to be sealed. Not only had Jacob stolen his birthright and his blessing, but Jacob had gained the favor of both his father and his mother, who despised Esau's choice of wives.

For some twenty years, Jacob worked for Laban—fourteen of those years in payment for marrying Laban's daughters, Leah and Rachel. Jacob the trickster actually was tricked by Laban into working an extra seven years for Rachel. During the two decades, Jacob's sons Reuben, Simeon, Levi, Judah, Dan, Naphtali, Gad, Asher, Issachar, Zebulun, and Joseph were born, as well as his daughter Dinah.

After fourteen years and with such a large family to support, Jacob had gone to Laban and had said, "You know how I have served you and how your livestock has been with me. For what you had before I came was little, and it has increased to a great amount; the LORD has blessed you since my coming. And now, when shall I also provide for my own house?" Laban asked Jacob what he wanted, and Jacob replied, in summary, "Let me have all of your speckled, spotted, and brown sheep and goats as my wages." Jacob then moved three days' journey away from Laban and developed his own herds and flocks. Jacob became "exceedingly prosperous." He had large flocks, many female and male servants, and camels and donkeys. (See Gen. 30.) Meanwhile, Laban's flocks grew weaker.

The day came when Jacob realized that Laban no longer looked with favor toward him. About that same time, the Lord said to Jacob, "Return to the land of your fathers and to your family, and I will be with you" (Gen. 31:3).

Jacob discovered a great truth about giants at that crisis point in his life. When you run from one giant, you often find yourself in the clutches of another one. The giants are at every turn, around every corner, behind every obstacle. You can never completely escape life's giants.

TWO CHOICES IN FACING A GIANT

When you face a giant, you have two choices: (1) to fight and expect to win, or (2) to run away, only to face another giant. In running from a giant, you are only delaying the showdown. You can face your giant today, with a willingness to take whatever wounds you receive, and go forward with victory and scars. Or you can run from the giant, become discouraged and faint in your heart, and then face a giant later—only in a weakened state. The more you run from giants, the weaker you become.

Fight the giants in your life now . . . in strength.
Or fight the giants later . . . in weakness.

Knowing that Laban was turning against him, and that Esau already had turned against him, Jacob no doubt felt as if he was between a rock and a hard place. Nevertheless, Jacob began the journey home. He "stole away," without telling Laban that he was leaving. Just as he had fled his home initially, Jacob fled from Laban under the cloak of secrecy.

Before Jacob got very far in his journey, Laban came after him. Showdown time had come for Jacob and one of his giants!

Laban accused Jacob not only of leaving without giving him an opportunity to say good-bye to his daughters and grandchildren but also of stealing the household idols. Jacob replied that he had left secretly because he was afraid of Laban, and he gave Laban permission to search for the idols.

■

Are you facing a giant?

■

When Laban did not find them, Jacob finally emerged from his grasshopper mentality and exerted giant-slaying authority. We are told that he rebuked Laban, saying, "What is my trespass? What is my sin?" He reminded Laban about how he had worked for him twenty years and hadn't stolen anything from him, how he had borne the loss of animals that had been killed by wild beasts, and how Laban had changed his wages ten times through the years. Finally, Jacob said, "Unless the God of my father, the God of Abraham and the Fear of Isaac, had been with me, surely now you would have sent me away empty-handed. God has seen my affliction and the labor of my hands, and rebuked you last night" (Gen. 31:42).

Laban backed down. One of Jacob's giants became as meek as one of Jacob's lambs. Laban offered to make a covenant with Jacob, and they parted in peace, with Laban kissing and blessing his daughters and grandchildren.

One giant down, and one to face.

As he neared his homeland, Jacob sent messengers to Esau to try to gain his favor. The messengers returned, saying, "We came to your brother Esau, and he also is coming to meet you, and four hundred men are with him" (Gen. 32:6).

Fear and distress gripped Jacob. He could not imagine any reason for his brother to descend upon him with four hundred men unless his brother intended to destroy him and his family. Jacob divided all the servants and flocks, herds, and camels in his entourage and sent them ahead in two groups—hoping that if Esau destroyed one group, the other group might escape.

He also prepared a great gift for Esau—two hundred female goats, twenty male goats, two hundred ewes and twenty rams, thirty milk camels and their colts, forty cows and ten bulls, twenty female donkeys and ten foals—all of which he commanded his servants to take to Esau.

Jacob prayed to the Lord, "Deliver me from the hand of my brother" (Gen. 32:11).

And finally, Jacob sent his wives, their servants, and his eleven sons and one daughter across the Jabbok. He remained on the other side of the brook, and there, all alone, Jacob unexpectedly came face-to-face with the *real* giant in his life, his perception of himself as a man who needed to trick his way to any success he might have.

The Bible tells us that a "Man" wrestled with Jacob all night. Jacob perceived that he had actually wrestled with God. In the course of that match, the Lord changed Jacob's name to Israel, which literally means "Prince with God." Jacob came out of that experience with two new beliefs embedded deep within his soul: he mattered to God, and he was destined to live. Jacob no longer needed to manipulate his way through life. He had the assurance that God was going to be with him as he faced his giants, and that God was going to fulfill the purpose He had for Jacob's life.

Just as Jacob had been warned, Esau arrived with four hundred men. Rather than confront Jacob with hatred, however, Esau "ran to meet him, and embraced him, and fell on his neck and kissed him, and they wept" (Gen. 33:4). God had changed Esau's heart, even to the point that Esau was reluctant to accept Jacob's peace offering, and he offered to provide extra protection for Jacob's flocks, herds, and family. The two brothers agreed to live in peace.

In all, Jacob faced three giants—Laban, Esau, and himself—and emerged a victor!

In facing the giant Laban, Jacob stood up for his rights and demanded that Laban deal with him fairly. And Laban agreed.

In facing the giant Esau, Jacob trusted in God to provide for him, and he obeyed God in returning home. And God changed Esau's heart.

In facing the giant of his own personality, Jacob wrestled with God and came to the conclusion that God not only could, but had, transformed him into a person with a new identity.

Jacob faced giants that represented his employer, his family, and his own personality. Each giant had a different hold on his life. But each giant became, at last, an ally and not an enemy.

WHICH GIANT INTIMIDATES YOU?

Are you facing a giant? Can you give that giant a name?

The Giant of Anxiety

As I travel this nation, I talk with people who tell me that they are living in a near constant state of worry. These people are facing a giant named anxiety.

They get up in the morning nervous about the day ahead. They go to bed at night, even after saying their prayers, and toss and turn as they think about what lies ahead and, even worse, what might lie ahead. Some have anxiety attacks on a regular basis, with palpitations of the heart, shortness of breath, and cold sweats. Others live in a state in which constant worry and dread lie just under the surface of all their other emotions.

Some of these people suffer from what I call *anxiety addiction*. They have fallen so deeply into the pattern and habit of worry that they don't feel right if they aren't worried about something. They have come to expect this inner state of turmoil and agitation as being normal for them. If they aren't worried about something, they think up something to worry about because joy and peace of heart are uncomfortable states for them. In other words, they think, *Surely something must be wrong for me to feel so good! I'd better worry about my happy state of mind!* It doesn't take long for this new worry to put them back into the state of anxiety to which they have become accustomed.

Anxiety is a giant. Many people are caught in its clutches.

The Giant of Rebellion

The giant of rebellion captures us when we set our minds and hearts to do something that we *know* is wrong to do. This giant has guilt built into it. We suffer because we want so desperately to enjoy doing what we know is wrong to do, but we are unable to enjoy ourselves fully. We go from one rebellious act to another, and in the process, we run into one giant after another.

> ■
> *Remind yourself that the Lord promised to take care of you.*
> ■

The Giant of Discouragement

A cycle of repeated failures can become a giant in our lives. Eventually, we feel trapped by failure. Just as Jacob did, we may feel as if we are working night and day and never getting ahead. Everywhere we look in our lives, we find things that aren't succeeding. The job goes sour; the marriage falls apart; we feel distant from God; our health begins to deteriorate. Before we know it, we're in the grips of the giant of discouragement, the years of failure overwhelming us.

The Giant of Poverty

"Lack" is a giant to many people. When we have obligations that far exceed our resources, we are in poverty. This state is not limited to finances. Poverty is a mind-set. It involves our feeling that we will never have enough, never be able to earn enough to pay the debt, never be able to support ourselves, never be able to get a grip on our giving and receiving habits.

Some people have a poverty of information. They don't even know what they don't know. Others have a poverty of love and affection. They deeply desire to know what it means to be valued and appreciated unconditionally by another person. Others are in the grip of the poverty of ability. They have no means of responding to life around them because they have no skills, no developed talents, no inner resources capable of facing life.

A MISSION TO BE FULFILLED

When we find ourselves in the clutches of giants such as these, we are wise if we do what Jacob did—cast ourselves totally and completely on the Lord and say to Him,

- "O God of my father Abraham and God of my father Isaac, the LORD who said to me, 'Return to your country and to your family, and I will deal well with you': I am not worthy of the least of all the mercies and of all the truth which You have shown Your servant; for I crossed over this Jordan with my staff, and now I have become two companies." Jacob came to the Lord with thanksgiving for what the Lord had done for him. He focused on God's past provision, not on his fear or sense of inadequacy. (See Gen. 32:9–10.) When we face a giant, we are wise to recount how the Lord has provided for us in the past.
- "Deliver me, I pray, from the hand of my brother, from the hand of Esau; for I fear him, lest he come and attack me and the mother with the children." Jacob expressed his fear to the Lord. He put his feelings into words and asked the Lord for His help. (See Gen. 32:11.) Don't be afraid to admit your weakness or feelings to the Lord.

- "For You said, 'I will surely treat you well, and make your descendants as the sand of the sea, which cannot be numbered for multitude.'" Jacob reminded the Lord, and himself, of God's promises to him. He put his sights on his future, not on his past or present. (See Gen. 32:12.)

Each of these prayers was answered for Jacob. The Lord continued to "deal well" with Jacob. He delivered him. He multiplied him.

Is there something that the Lord has compelled you, commanded you, or convicted you to do? Is there something that He has promised you? God's Word is filled with commandments and promises. Take them personally, recognizing that they do apply to you. God provides what we need in order for us to do what He asks. See yourself today as having marching orders from God and the provision you need to carry them out!

Remind yourself that the Lord asked you to take a particular action. Remind yourself that the Lord promised to take care of you. Ask Him to make His presence real to you now, to give you both the courage and the comfort to take the action you need to take.

And then, face up to your giant. Do it without delay.

Counselors frequently report that their clients who have been victims of abuse begin to get well only after they have had a confrontation with the abuser—a confrontation in which they can respond to the abuser not as a victim, but as a person with authority and power.

In school, we have found that students who suffer from test anxiety get over their fear only after they are helped and guided to take a test and pass it.

The old commonsense adage that you need to get right back on the horse that throws you is good advice for nearly every area of life.

If we don't confront our giants immediately, we will face them again unless God sovereignly removes them from our lives.

Think back to Moses for a moment. Moses spent forty years on the back side of a wilderness because he killed an Egyptian who brutally mistreated one of his fellow Hebrews. Moses knew that Pharaoh would search for him to kill him. Pharaoh became a giant in Moses' life. And Moses ran from him.

But Moses did not rid Pharaoh from his life until he confronted him in the power of the Lord. Moses faced other giants in the interim, but his first giant never went away. It was to Pharaoh that the Lord sent Moses with the message: "Let My people go." As much as he didn't want to go, Moses had to return to Egypt and square off against Pharaoh for his own destiny to be fulfilled in the Lord and for God's people to be delivered.

Moses faced Pharaoh not just one time but many times. Each time Moses made the same request: "Let us go to worship the Lord." Each time the answer from Pharaoh was the same: "No."

In the course of confronting Pharaoh, Moses was wounded and scarred. His own people began to blame him for the extra persecution they received. We have no indication in the story of the Exodus that Moses was exempt from all the plagues that came upon Egypt as the result of the Lord's word spoken through him. Confronting the giant of Pharaoh wasn't easy for Moses.

The Lord, however, honored Moses' obedience and courage in facing Pharaoh, and He stepped in and caused such overwhelming devastation to Pharaoh and the families of the Egyptians that Pharaoh relented and let the Hebrew people leave Egypt—but only temporarily. After several days, Pharaoh sent his chariots and soldiers in hot pursuit of Moses and the children of Israel.

As the children of Israel found themselves with the Red Sea before them and the army of Pharaoh behind them, they became afraid. They cried out, "Because there were no graves in Egypt, have you taken us away to die in the wilderness? . . .

It would have been better for us to serve the Egyptians than that we should die in the wilderness."

Moses responded to the people with giant-slaying wisdom. He said, "Do not be afraid. Stand still, and see the salvation of the LORD, which He will accomplish for you today. For the Egyptians whom you see today, you shall see again no more forever. The LORD will fight for you, and you shall hold your peace." (See Exod. 14:10–24.)

Moses had personally faced down the giant of Pharaoh. Moses knew that this giant was vulnerable, that God was on his side, that God had delivered the people from the death angel at the time of the Passover, and that God was bigger than Pharaoh.

THE GIANT'S POWER OVER US IS DESTROYED

You may still have to live with, work with, worship with, or serve with the person who has caused you to have grasshopper mentality. But you no longer need to cower in fear before him.

You may still have to see the person who has bullied or abused you. But you no longer need to be intimidated.

You may still have to do business with, or have dealings with, the person who has ridiculed or insulted you. But you no longer need to have your self-esteem affected by her or allow her hurtful words to injure you.

You can look at your former giant and say, "You may not be destroyed. But your power over me has been destroyed. Do what you will. I won't be afraid of you, bow to you, or be influenced by you in a negative way."

AN ABILITY TO SAY, "YOU CAN COUNT ON ME"

Sometimes our giants come against our families, our neighborhoods, our churches, our communities, or our civic groups. Being willing to face a giant, and to risk wounds and scars in the process, means that we are willing to say to those who are facing a giant with us, "You can count on me. I'm not afraid to do my part in facing this giant."

The giants we face as a nation, and on a smaller scale, as communities and cities, tend to be the giants of crime, poverty, homelessness, and ignorance. None of us can take on a giant of this magnitude and defeat it in one blow as David did with Goliath. But when we join with others of like mind and courage, we can face the giant as it manifests itself in our immediate community and defeat it.

A young girl in my biology class in the 1960s taught me this lesson.

As the holiday season neared, she suggested that we do something as a class for a needy family. I thought that was a great idea, and I countersuggested that we get the entire high school of 1,500 students involved. I set about to enlist the support of other teachers and coaches, and before the campaign was over, we had raised $1,500 for the project.

Sometimes we are required to give our all.

The students identified families to be assisted and spent many hours buying presents and food for them, trying to stretch that $1,500 as far as it could possibly go. They did an amazing job.

We were scheduled to deliver gifts and food on Christmas Eve, and frankly, I didn't want to go. I would have preferred to spend that special night with my wife and sons, but after much persuasion, I went with a group of students. The deliveries took us far back into rural areas outside Birmingham, Alabama.

At one stop, we entered a backwoods shack where all we found was one pitiful little flame from an oil lamp giving light to the house. The walls were covered with cardboard. The floor was sawdust. In the house were three beautiful children, an attractive but very tired-looking and sallow-skinned mother, and a thirty-six-year-old father who was gaunt, marked with the ravages of a terminal illness.

The students never sang Christmas carols more beautifully

than they did that night in that backwoods shack. I saw true joy and happiness in their faces, and in the faces of those to whom we had brought gifts. Tears began streaking down the face of the father as he repeatedly thanked us. In his zeal to do something in return, he went over to an old-fashioned icebox and took a dressed rabbit from it, apparently the meal he had intended for their Christmas dinner, and offered it to us. We declined and assured him that ours was the pleasure to give and share, and then we all bowed our knees on that sawdust floor and said a prayer of thanks to God.

No, we hadn't reversed poverty in the world, in our state, in our county, or even in the life of that family. But we had reversed it for a few moments! We had infused hope and joy into lives of people who had little hope and little joy. We had stared down a giant, even for a little while, on a Christmas Eve.

And we walked away from that home knowing two things. One, we knew that we had won. Our hearts and lives had been touched and changed. We had received more than we had given, which is always the way genuine giving works with God. A giant of despair, discouragement, fear, and lack had been faced down that night and defeated.

The other lesson we learned was that together we had made a difference in tackling a giant in our world. None of us would have, or perhaps even could have, taken on that giant alone. But together, we had won a victory.

Some giants require that we give our time. Others our talents. Others our money and goods. Still others our words of hope and enthusiastic encouragement. Sometimes we are required to give our all. If we are willing to bear a few of the scars, however, we can become winners in the land of giants.

CHAPTER 8

The Invisible Heartbeat of Success

I t's an old story, that of an ad in the newspaper for a lost dog. It read:

REWARD—LOST DOG! Mixed breed, only three legs, blind in the left eye, and nearly deaf. Answers to the name "Lucky."

Lucky must have been quite a dog with a terrific disposition for his owner to offer a reward and to go to the trouble of taking out an ad in the newspaper. You have to believe that if Lucky could speak, he would say, "I make the most of all that comes, and the least of all that goes."

Do you feel lucky today?

It all depends on your attitude, doesn't it?

Attitudes are the invisible heartbeat of our minds. Just as the heart sends out blood to nourish and cleanse every part of our bodies so that we can function at our maximum potential, so our attitudes cause our minds to take in certain information, reject other information, and cause us to function mentally in ways that bring us to success.

Attitudes are more important than facts. They are controlling valves for our behavior. Over time, we have attitudes that become so deeply embossed on our minds that they are like mental and emotional habits. We think in certain ways because we have chosen to view life in a certain way over time.

We become not only what we think but *how we think about what we think*. Attitude is the value and the positive-or-negative charge that we add to opinion. Attitudes have both direction and strength.

Think of a magnet for a moment. Before that hunk of metal was magnetized, it was neutral. Once it was given a charge, it attracted particles to it. Your attitude will attract ideas to it. Unlike metal magnets, however, attitudinal magnets attract like qualities. A positive attitude attracts positive ideas and positive opinions. A negative attitude attracts negative ideas and negative opinions.

Attitudes also produce behavior of like kind. Positive attitudes result in positive behavior. The stronger the attitude, the more likely the behavior. In other words, the more positive your attitude, the more positive your behavior.

Negative attitudes produce negative behavior, and in like manner, the stronger the attitude, the more likely the negative behavior.

We don't need a barely positive attitude to survive and conquer in today's world. We need a strong positive attitude. The stronger the heartbeat, the stronger the body. The stronger the positive attitude, the greater the motivation toward success in facing giants.

> ■
> *Attitudes are more important than facts.*
> ■

Emerson said, "A man is what he thinks all day long. The key to every man is his thoughts."

Marcus Aurelius, a Roman philosopher, said, "The world in which we live is determined by our thoughts."

Virgil, the great Roman poet, said, "They can because they think they can."

George Russell, an Irish poet, said, "We become what we contemplate."

When we begin to think that it is possible for us to slay giants, we take on giants and win.

What are some of the attitudes, then, that make up giant-slaying thinking? There are at least four.

FOUR COMPONENTS OF
GIANT-SLAYING THINKING

One of the things that I taught my science students years ago was a basic scientific principle that no two objects can occupy the same space at the same time. The same goes for our attitudes and thoughts. We cannot think two thoughts at the same time. We cannot hold two opposite attitudes at the same time. We can't harbor positive and negative emotions at the same time.

For each positive component that makes up giant-slaying thinking, there's a negative one that contributes to grasshopper mentality. We aren't going to focus on the negatives here, but it's important for you to recognize that they exist. In other words, if you don't emphasize the ideas and attitudes that lead to giant-slaying thinking, you may very well be developing grasshopper mentality. Go with the positives!

Component #1: Face Today's Giant Today

I remember walking down a dirt road to church with my grandfather when I was only ten years old. I told my grandfather that I could hardly wait until I was sixteen so I could quit school and get a job. He said, "Son, don't wish your life away. It will pass by very fast." Those were words of wisdom I am just now old enough to appreciate!

What you do today is important.

Many of us put off slaying some of the giants in our lives in hopes that they will go away, or that we will somehow grow in our ability to slay a particular giant at a future time. Today's giants need to be faced and defeated today.

Giants that are left alone grow.

If you have a bad habit that needs to be cleansed from your life, delaying action will only make that habit harder to break. If you are letting something slide, even though you know that it needs to be dealt with, delaying the confrontation will only make the confrontation more difficult.

Don't allow yourself to live in the past, wishing you were back in Egypt where the giants were ones you already knew how to bow down to. Don't allow yourself to live in the future, hoping that you'll get to a place where you won't have any giants at all. Deal with the giants that are before you today.

Two very successful football coaches, the late Paul "Bear" Bryant of the University of Alabama and Lou Holtz of Notre Dame, have carried the following poem by an unknown author in their billfolds:

> This is the beginning of a new day. God has given me this day to use as I will.
> I can waste it or use it for good. What I do today is important, because I'm exchanging a day of my life for it.
> When tomorrow comes, this day will be gone forever, leaving something I have traded for it.
> I want it to be gain, not loss; good, not evil; success, not failure; in order that I shall not regret the price I paid for it.

Have an attitude that now is the time, today is the day, right away is the moment to capture.

Component #2: Choose to Be a Nice Person

We've all heard the saying, "Nice guys finish last." It isn't true. Nice guys may get beat up from time to time, but ultimately, nice guys have the things that are truly important to have: health, a loving family and friends, a faith that's strong, and peace of heart and mind.

Ask a person what the most important things in life are, and you're going to find intangibles: love, joy, peace, faith, hope. Although many of us spend a great deal of time pursuing tangibles—jobs, houses, cars, gadgets, powerful positions, and important careers—it is the intangibles that we can't do without.

Ask a person who has a life-threatening illness what he wants most in life and it isn't a promotion.

Ask the person who has a missing runaway child what she wants most in life and it isn't a new car.

Ask the person who has just been through a painful divorce what he wants most in life and it isn't a VCR with remote control.

Nice guys are able to go to bed at night and get a full night's sleep, knowing that all is well with them and the world. Nice guys have a house full of warm family fellowship at holiday times. Nice guys have a smile on their faces that is genuine and relaxed.

I once gave the presentation "Being Nice to People" in Pennsylvania. After my talk, a man by the last name of Doctor came up on the platform and told me he had a story to share with me.

Mr. Doctor's wife worked in a state prison, and after returning from a weeklong vacation, she was called into the office of the warden. The warden proceeded to tell her that numerous inmates had asked about her while she was away. They wanted to make certain she was all right, and not ill or injured. The officials said they had never had prisoners ask about a prison employee in the way the prisoners had asked about Mrs. Doctor.

One of the guards found the prisoners' behavior to be curious so he asked a group of inmates why they were so interested in Mrs. Doctor. The prisoners were very responsive and said, "Mrs. Doctor is nice to us. She treats us like we are human beings." When the prison officials passed that word on to Mrs. Doctor, she said, "I just practice the golden rule. Everybody wants to be *somebody*, even a prisoner."

Being nice to people means listening to them, treating them with respect, upholding their dignity, doing some of the things they want to do when they want to do them, and finding ways to lighten their load and give them joy.

Being nice to people means having manners and extending courtesy to others.

Being nice to people means greeting people with a smile

and calling them by name, recognizing their individuality, and expressing delight that they are a part of your life.

Being nice to people means bridling your anger and controlling your tongue, recognizing that words can and do hurt others.

Do nice guys kill giants? Consider these words in Romans 12:17–21:

■ *Take time to do the job right.* ■

> Repay no one evil for evil. Have regard for good things in the sight of all men. If it is possible, as much as depends on you, live peaceably with all men. Beloved, do not avenge yourselves, but rather give place to wrath; for it is written, "Vengeance is Mine, I will repay," says the Lord. Therefore
>
> > "If your enemy is hungry, feed
> > him;
> > If he is thirsty, give him a drink;
> > For in so doing you will heap
> > coals of fire on his head."
>
> Do not be overcome by evil, but overcome evil with good.

Some menacing giants just may be turned into gentle giants by your kindness. As Abraham Lincoln once said, "You slay an enemy by making him your friend."

Component #3: Do Your Best Every Day

At a workshop conducted by the Power of Positive Students International Foundation, I met a fifth grade teacher who told me about a boy she had in her class the previous year. Joshua was hyperactive, and this teacher had worked hard with him to help him become the best student he could be.

At the end of the year, she told Joshua that she was moving on to teach sixth grade and that she hoped she would have Joshua in her class the following year so they could continue the good work they had begun.

During the summer, tragedy struck and Joshua died. As she and Joshua's mother talked together after the funeral, Joshua's mother told how Joshua had talked about his teacher at the dinner table. Joshua had told his family about his teacher's multiple sclerosis and about how hard she had to work to overcome her personal difficulties every day. He had concluded, "She comes to school every day and she gives her best, so I have to give my best, too."

Our attitudes aren't fixed. They can change from day to day. Each day, we need to get up and say to ourselves, "I'm going to have the very best attitude I can have today. I'm going to give my best to the tasks that lie before me."

One of the main reasons why people don't have an "I'm going to do my best today" attitude is that they don't think they've got what it takes to do a good job. The result is that they don't try as hard and don't do all they are capable of doing. The result of that behavior, of course, is that the job they do isn't their best, so it can never be a truly good job!

When was the last time you sat down and counted your blessings?

When I was attending West End Baptist Church in Birmingham, Alabama, I had the privilege of hearing Dwight Moody preach on the radio. He told a story about an incident that happened shortly after he started preaching. He had preached the best sermon he knew to preach, and a number of people had really been blessed by it. After the service, however, a local English teacher came up to him and said, "You had a nice sermon, but you made twenty-six grammatical errors."

Moody was dumbstruck for a few moments, not knowing how to respond. Finally, he felt as if the Lord had dropped these words into his mouth: "Well, ma'am, I'm doing the best I can with what I've got. Are you?"

I've always remembered that. His response was what my grandmother had instilled in me when she taught me how to push a lawn mower, hoe her sweet potatoes, and gather vegetables from her garden. She often said, "A job that's done right is a job you can be proud of."

Do your best. Take time to do the job right. Your best may not be the best that somebody else can do. But when you do your best, it's enough, no matter what anybody else does.

Grasshopper mentality says, "I can't," "I won't," and "I don't care."

Giant slayers have an attitude of "I can," "I will," and "I care—about others and about myself."

Component #4: Be Thankful

One of the most positive attitudes is perhaps best described as having a thankful heart.

Are you grateful for the good things that come your way? Do you call to your remembrance the good times of your past and express your thankfulness to God for His provision to you, His deliverance of you, and the gracious gifts and blessings that He has given to you?

In 1620, about a hundred men and women came to America and created a settlement called Plymouth. Their first winter was an incredibly bitter one. Death took a heavy toll. By the end of the first year, more of their number were in the cemetery than were gathered around the common dinner tables. Food was running very low. Governor Bradford began issuing just five grains of corn to each person for a day's ration. For more than a month, each person in Plymouth had only five grains of corn to eat a day!

The fortunes of the settlers changed with the spring weather and the peace they forged with the Native Americans. For many years, however, Governor Bradford took the opportunity at their annual Thanksgiving meal to remind the settlers of God's faithfulness in providing for them in the past by placing five grains of corn beside each plate.

When was the last time you sat down and counted your blessings, naming them one by one? When we do so, we find ourselves in awe at the many ways God has provided for us. We see life and our daily problems from a different perspective.

When we recall how the Lord has delivered us from past giants, we grow in confidence that He will deliver us from the giants we are facing today.

When we recall how the Lord provided a way and means for us in the past, we grow in confidence that He can remove any obstacle that stands in our path toward success.

When we recall how the Lord has helped us to overcome difficulties, we grow in confidence that today's difficulty will be a part of tomorrow's thanksgiving.

A RENEWED ATTITUDE EVERY MORNING

A Catholic nun in Red Bud, Illinois, once handed me a card with Psalm 118:24 on it: "This is the day the LORD has made; we will rejoice and be glad in it." My granddaughter, Michelle, and I often recite that verse to each other.

The fact is, each new day is a gift from God. He makes each day, and our proper response is to rejoice and be glad.

God's mercies are new every morning. (See Lam. 3:23.) That means He has something new and wonderful for us each day.

That same verse in the Bible tells this about God: "Great is Your faithfulness." God is going to be with us as we face every moment of today.

When we really grasp those two truths—God has something good for us, and God is going to be there to help us—we have absolutely no excuse for having a bad attitude!

Our attitude, however, is something that we constantly must guard. Proverbs 4:23 advises, "Keep your heart with all diligence, for out of it spring the issues of life." We need to watch how we think and feel about things—that's what it means to "keep our hearts." In other words, we need to keep a constant watch on our attitudes. Our attitudes will affect the most important things in our lives.

Watch your thoughts; they become words.
Watch your words; they become actions.
Watch your actions; they become habits.
Watch your habits; they become your character.
Watch your character; it becomes your destiny.

Your attitudes are your invisible heartbeat, the very well-spring, of your entire life—for good or bad, for success or failure.

Is it possible to be a winner in the land of giants with a defeated, down, grasshopper-mentality attitude? I doubt it.

Does your future hinge on the attitudes you have today? I believe it does!

CHAPTER 9

The Invisible
Giant
of Fear

Many coaches and players have known the stinging pain of losing a game primarily because the home team was more scared of the opponent than the opponent was scared of the home team. Teams rarely do well if they play scared. Rather, they do well if they play "scarier"—believing themselves to be the meanest, baddest, biggest, toughest, smartest, quickest, and best team on the field.

The coin of confidence always has two sides: faith and fear.

Faith is best placed in God, not oneself. He is the One who knows all, can do all, and is never too late or too early. He alone has all wisdom and knowledge and resources. Within that broader context of faith, however, a person can feel confident. Paul perhaps has said it best: "I can do all things through Christ who strengthens me" (Phil. 4:13).

Self-confidence lies primarily in knowing these things about yourself as you ponder a particular decision or take up a challenge:

1. I've prepared myself for this challenge, developing my skills and talents as best I know how.

2. I have researched the solutions, outcomes, or answers as best I know how.
3. I have the resources or ability to contact resources that I perceive may be necessary should I need help beyond myself.
4. I believe this particular opportunity or challenge is something worthy of my time, talent, and resources.
5. I have calculated the risks as best as I can.
6. And most important of all, I'm associated with the One who has strengths to fill in the gaps of all my remaining weaknesses.

When we have prepared ourselves, anticipated the outcomes, and believe in something, we are many steps ahead of most people when it comes to having the confidence it takes to slay a giant.

Before we slay an external giant, however, we very often need to slay an internal one: fear.

THE INTERNAL ENEMY OF FEAR

Fear is rarely focused, which is part of its nature. Fear is rooted in "I don't know" and "I don't understand" far more than in "I know" or "I believe."

Sometimes the fear is a fear of failure. It may be a fear of embarrassment or a fear of loss. The most debilitating thing about this type of fear is that it prevents us from reaching out for things we might be able to achieve. This type of fear paralyzes.

Fear compels us to think, *If I don't do this, I'll stay alive, and everything will be all right.* Unfortunately, fear disables us to the point that we may be alive, but rarely is everything all right. The person who is paralyzed into doing nothing quickly stagnates and takes no risks. Such a person doesn't grow. Life without growth and risk is not much of a life!

Fear of failure actually leads us to accept failure as not only

■ *Faith is best placed in God, not oneself.* ■

inevitable but acceptable. When that happens, grasshopper mentality is firmly entrenched.

Both faith and fear can become cyclical. The more we exercise our faith and reach out for something better, higher, and nobler in our lives, the more we succeed. The stronger our faith becomes at that point, the more likely we are to reach out for something even better, higher, and nobler. The fear cycle is vicious: fear produces failure, and failure increases fear.

A MISSED OPPORTUNITY

I once missed a great opportunity because I allowed fear to replace faith.

My wife, Carolyn, and I had driven to Hilton Head Island to spend a weekend. Hilton Head is a beautiful resort area off the coast of South Carolina, and part of the reason we were going there was to explore the idea of purchasing a vacation home.

> ■
> *Logic,
> reasoning,
> and evidence
> all tend to
> fold in the
> face of fear.*
> ■

As we drove toward the island, we talked about how our goals in life had changed over the years. One of us remarked that it had been only a few years ago that we had established a financial goal of earning $10,000 a year, and there we were, thinking about investing in a condominium on that beautiful island.

I had read numerous books on positive thinking, and they all encouraged "thinking big." Carolyn and I figured it was about time that we started to think BIG as well as to take our accountant's advice and invest.

When we arrived at Hilton Head, we called a friend who was a real estate agent and had promised to show us some bargain-priced property. He took us to one particular condominium and said, "Billy, if it were not for the recent recession and its effect on the real estate market, this place we're looking at would sell for about $220,000 to $225,000. As it is, you can buy it right now for only $125,000." All that we had to do was put down $25,000 and mortgage the remaining $100,000. He felt certain that in a year or so, when the market picked up again, we would be able to sell it for $75,000 to $100,000 more than we had paid for it. In the meantime, the condominium could be leased to other vacationers whose payments would cover the monthly mortgage.

As a schoolteacher, the only time I dealt with figures such as those was in math class! I became truly excited. Carolyn and I talked it over briefly and decided to buy the condo, gratefully signing the contract and giving the real estate agent a check. We felt as if we were on cloud nine for the rest of the weekend. We also felt very fortunate to have a friend who could point us toward such a great deal.

On Sunday evening as we drove home, my wife said, "Billy, do you think we've done the right thing?" We began to talk about what would happen if I lost my job, if we were unable to rent the condo, or if the recession deepened.

Before we knew it, the list of possible hazards seemed endless. Seeds of doubt sprouted quickly, and by the time we arrived at our home, I had a gnawing feeling that I had done the wrong thing.

The first thing I did upon entering our house was to call the real estate agent at Hilton Head. I explained our apprehension. I told him that I had always believed that if a person did not feel good inside about a decision, he should not have made it. The end result of the conversation was that I asked my friend to tear up the contract and return our check. He told me he thought I was making a terrible mistake, but he would do whatever I asked.

A year later, Carolyn and I went back to Hilton Head for another visit. We arrived to find that during the year, real estate sales had turned sharply upward. Our friend told us he hated to say "I told you so" as he showed us his ledger. The condo we had almost purchased had recently sold for a cool $220,000—$95,000 more than we would have paid for it.

Looking at the figures before me, I felt almost physically

sick with regret. Ninety-five thousand dollars was more money than I had made during the first ten years of my teaching and coaching career combined. The news spoiled our weekend, and as I recall, we left for home earlier than we had planned.

When I thought back over what happened, I realized that my fear about the purchase had caused me totally to dismiss several key facts:

- I had the money for the down payment that was required.
- I was employed. If I lost my job, I had a good track record and lots of skills and training. In all likelihood, I could have been hired someplace else rather quickly.
- We may not have been able to make several months of ongoing mortgage payments, but we probably could have made one or two payments—long enough to find out how to get people to sublease the condo.

The point was and is, fear is not rational. Fear is reactive; it is rooted in our emotions, and it excites our emotions. Once fear has taken hold, we are rarely capable of focusing our thinking. Logic, reasoning, and evidence all tend to fold in the face of fear.

I said to my wife, "Carolyn, let's make a pact never again to fill each other's head with doubt and fear that will keep us from doing things we can do and want to do." By the following weekend, I had decided the best way to conquer fear was to take action. Carolyn and I drove to Myrtle Beach, which was closer to our home than Hilton Head. There we found a condominium we could afford, and we bought it! That was more than ten years ago, by the way, and we have never been sorry we made that purchase.

Fear and self-doubt are paralyzing. Faith and self-confidence are mobilizing.

The only way to break out of a cycle of fear is to take action. Do something as an expression of your faith in God and faith in your preparation and enthusiasm. Act on the opportunities that present themselves.

Of course, not all opportunities are worth taking. That's where your preparation will help you sift out good opportunities from not-so-good ones. Trust your abilities, rooted in your faith that God will help you discern and make wise choices as you ask questions, weigh options, and look for hidden dangers. In the end, if you firmly believe you are looking at a risk worth taking and a challenge worth pursuing, go for it!

Wishing and hoping don't make things happen. Planning, preparing, committing, and then taking action—those are the keys to moving forward.

UNCHECKED FEAR PRODUCES PANIC

Fear that is allowed to run wild, go unchecked, and remain unbridled is fear that turns into panic. Panic is the feeling of being out of control.

In March 1984, my wife and I decided to drive to Myrtle Beach, South Carolina, from our home in Cumberland, Maryland, so we might spend a few days basking on the beach. The snow was just melting off the streets in Maryland, and the sun was shining brightly.

Shortly after we were on the highway, Carolyn cautioned me to be on the lookout for icy spots that might still be on the roads. I confess that I did not heed her advice.

As we approached the top of a mountain, snow began to fall lightly. When we started descending, the car suddenly hit an icy spot and went totally out of control. We found ourselves moving across both lanes of the highway, totally helpless to do anything except hope and pray that we survived the moment. Although the entire episode lasted only a few seconds, it seemed like an eternity. Thoughts raced through my mind as numerous and swirling as the snowflakes coming from the sky: *Would we crash through the guardrails? Would*

Act on the opportunities that present themselves.

another vehicle hit us? Would we be injured? Should I attempt to steer the vehicle? What about applying the brakes?

There was no time to take action on any of my thoughts. They were out-of-control thoughts just as the vehicle in which we were riding was out of control.

Amazingly, our automobile straightened on its own without our turning over or hitting either a guardrail or another vehicle. I was able to stop the car safely so that we might regain our equilibrium before starting again on our journey.

Believe me, for the next seven hours of the trip, I gave a great deal of thought to the possibility of icy patches on the road. I drove much more cautiously and slowly.

There is a degree of fear that is healthy fear. This fear has been built into us by our Creator so that we might preserve our lives and fulfill His destiny for us. This fear causes us to keep our children from wandering into streets. This fear compels us to keep laws, including God's divine laws. This fear leads to life. If I had had a little more healthy fear as I drove, we may not have spun out of control and experienced the unhealthy fear of panic.

Panic is fear that keeps us from fulfilling God's destiny for our lives. It is so paralyzing that we fail to grab hold of all the blessings God sends our way. Ultimately, it is a fear that leads to death.

How is it that some people come to live in a state of panic? I believe it's because they allow themselves to become detached from the Source of their faith.

NOT GOOD IF DETACHED

As I prepared to attend a football game one Saturday, I noticed these words printed on my ticket: NOT GOOD IF DETACHED. In other words, if the stub of the ticket had become detached prior to my presenting the ticket to the usher at the stadium, I would not be allowed to enter. Even though I had paid for my ticket, I would not be allowed to see the game. My seat in the stands would be empty all for the want of a 1-by-1½-inch piece of printed lightweight cardboard!

We are vulnerable to fear when we allow ourselves to become detached from the Source of our self-confidence, the Lord Himself.

THE SPIN-OFFS OF CRIPPLING FEAR

Fear by itself is a potent force driving us toward grasshopper mentality. It has a number of close relatives that keep us from reaching our potential in all areas of life. Among the first-cousin enemies of fear are procrastination, overwork, time-wasters, confusion, and perfectionism, which you may never have associated with fear before.

Procrastination

Procrastination—putting off until tomorrow what should be done today—is often a manifestation of fear. We stall and stall because we are afraid of taking action. What are we afraid of?

Sometimes it's a fear of doing the wrong thing or of making the wrong choice. Sometimes it's a fear that there may be no need for us in the future if we finish the current job. Sometimes it's a fear that we aren't able to finish the job.

As an educator, I have seen numerous students procrastinate in completing an assignment because they knew that after they turned in the assignment, it would be graded. I suspect that same fear underlies much procrastination among employees and others. Jobs and tasks aren't evaluated until they are completed. The fear is, *What if I didn't do it right? What might my punishment be?* Those who think this way are usually unsure of their skills and abilities and are fearful of being weighed in the scales and found wanting.

If you are a habitual procrastinator, ask yourself, Why am I afraid to get this job done?

You cannot be a procrastinator if you expect to become a winner in the land of giants. Giant slayers are action-oriented people. They don't run away from challenges or ignore them; they welcome the opportunity to fill a larger cup. Have you fallen into the habit of putting off tasks or goals? What is it you want to do that you haven't accomplished, or more important, what is keeping you from doing what you want to do?

Procrastinators who want to become doers should consider these steps:

- Admit that you are a procrastinator.
- Have the desire to stop procrastinating.
- Believe that you can, with God's help, break the habit.
- Resolve to get into the habit of action.
- Accomplish tasks daily that will permit you to experience success.
- Think about the good feelings you get when you experience success.
- Associate with action-oriented people.

Be determined to change from a procrastinator to an action-oriented person, and stay focused on doing what you truly want to do. Begin to practice taking action by establishing attainable, measurable, short-term goals and achieving them. Get into the action habit.

Overwork

Work is healthy, and I love doing it. I've worked hard all my life, and I still enjoy putting in a full day of mental and physical effort. But for some people, work is an obsession. They push themselves to do and do and do. They never "turn off" at the end of a day. They continue to drive themselves to work longer hours, usually at an increasingly frenetic pace, until the day comes when they collapse.

What's behind overwork? Very often it is a fear of not living up to another person's expectations or a fear that if they say no to a particular task or project, they will be ridiculed, lose face, or never be hired again.

A freelance artist told me that in the first few years of being in business on her own, she repeatedly had to fight the urge to work weekends. She found it very difficult to say no to a prospective client. She said, "I had heard how difficult it was to be in business for yourself. Everybody said to me that being an independent artist was a feast-or-famine proposition, and I knew I couldn't afford famine. I thought, *I have to say yes to every job that comes along; otherwise I might starve.* As a result, I took on way too much work. Eventually, I was working fourteen- and sixteen-hour days, but I still didn't think I could say no to a client who demanded a rush job. I was so frightened of famine that I was gorging on my own feast!

"The day came when I could hardly get out of bed, I was so exhausted. I ended up spending nearly two weeks just sleeping. I only had enough energy to pick up the phone and call other artist friends to take over the projects I still had to do. My body had had enough of my mind's foolishness, and no matter how much I wanted to work, I couldn't.

"When I finally got my energy back, I went back to the drawing board in more ways than one. I decided that taking weekends was a required part of staying in business. And I also discovered that I still was able to stay busy forty to fifty hours a week."

A pattern of overwork is often driven by a lack of faith in God to provide what we need. Workaholics truly are addicted to work. They can't imagine life that isn't framed by deadlines and to-do lists. If you fall into that category, I suggest that you start scheduling some downtime for yourself. If you must put it on a schedule, do so. Give yourself at least two or three hours a week in which you refuse to schedule anything. Let those hours be times for spontaneous activity, rest, and recreation. Decide at the last minute what you are going to do with your rest time. Consider it a preventive measure for your health. Gradually increase the number of hours that you give to yourself in a week for recreation.

Always keep in mind that the word *recreation* is actually

re-creation. This is your time to create again the physical energy and pool of ideas that you need to have to become a giant slayer.

Don't be afraid to trust God to supply your need. In saying no to overobligation of your time and energy, you may actually be saying yes to Him, giving God room and time to speak to you, lead you, and guide you in ways that will make you even more effective and efficient.

Time-Wasters

A number of things in our lives don't flow from fear but contribute to fear. When we waste time on trivial, unimportant activities, we often face deadlines and obligations somewhat unexpectedly—to the point where we panic or feel fear that we aren't going to be able to succeed. It's like the little boy said after he fell, "The floor came up to hit me real fast."

It's like the person who wastes time getting to the station and then has to run for the train as it starts pulling away from the platform. The meandering stroll to the station may have appeared relaxing, but it certainly isn't worth the rush of adrenaline that one feels in barely making it on board.

Life has lots of time-wasters, among them:

- Unimportant phone calls
- Long lines
- Machinery that doesn't work properly
- Unnecessary memos
- Traffic jams
- Most television programs
- Waiting rooms

At the end of a day engaged in such activities—even if there is a certain amount of enjoyment in some of them—a person is likely to feel panic that he hasn't done anything that truly needed to be done. At the end of a life engaged in such activities, a person is likely to feel a deep-seated fear that he hasn't fulfilled his destiny.

As much as is possible, isolate the time-wasters in your life and map out a plan to avoid them.

I heard of a man who lived in a big city with massive traffic problems during rush hours. He decided to go into work each day at 4:30 A.M. in his jogging suit, carrying his suit in a suit bag along with his briefcase. Once at the office, he jogged two blocks away to a gym that opened at 5:00 A.M., where he worked out until 6:00 A.M., then showered and dressed for the day. He walked another two blocks to a restaurant where he had breakfast, read the morning paper, and organized his workday. He was in his office by 7:00 A.M., giving him a full hour's head start in writing memos and working on reports before his colleagues arrived and the phone started to ring.

That hour at the beginning of the day put him in good shape for leaving work at 2:00 P.M., which he did, with his employer's permission. On some days, he stopped by the library, which was on the way to the parking garage where he kept his car. At the library, he picked up books on tape, and he listened to them as he drove to and from work. He made it home by 3:00 P.M. in time to plug in his computer and work from his home office until 5:00 or 6:00 P.M. While his colleagues were battling traffic, he was enjoying dinner and a relaxing time with his family. The entire family went to bed at 8:30 to 9:00 P.M. They rarely turned on the television set, by the way. The children worked on homework and the parents read in the evenings. An early bedtime made it easy for him to get up at 3:45 the next morning.

This man rarely stood in lines or lost time in traffic. He made the most of his work hours and led a full and balanced life. Rather than waste time, he used time. And the result was that he hardly knew what it meant to feel stress about a deadline.

Confusion

Panic is nearly always associated with confusion. And wherever a spirit of confusion reigns, we can know that evil is afoot. Paul wrote to Timothy, "God has not given us a spirit of fear, but of power and of love and of a sound mind" (2 Tim. 1:7). A sound mind is free of confusion.

If you are in a confusing situation, ask the Lord for discernment. Get to the root of what is causing the constant state of upheaval or disorientation. Then, either eliminate the source of confusion, or leave the scene. Giants will roar at you to try to confuse you and cause you to panic. That's what lions do. They circle their prey and roar. The animal they are preying upon hears the roars, coming first from this direction and then that, and becomes confused and disoriented, not knowing which way to turn. In fear, the animal panics. And at that point, the lions in the pride attack.

According to 1 Peter 5:8, "the devil walks about like a roaring lion, seeking whom he may devour." Peter then challenges us to "resist him, steadfast in the faith" (v. 9).

After you have discerned the root cause of the confusion around you, ask the Holy Spirit to impart peace to your heart and a sense of order to your mind. First Corinthians 14:33 asserts, "God is not the author of confusion but of peace." Paul also wrote to the Corinthians, "Let all things be done decently and in order" (1 Cor. 14:40).

Giants are rarely slain by confused people.

Perfectionism

Finally, fear is linked closely to perfectionism. Perfectionism is the desire to do everything in an A+ fashion, without any error. It is rooted in a personal fear of failure—including a fear that we won't be loved, included, appreciated, or valued if we make mistakes or fail to live up to the highest standards.

When the Bible calls for us to be perfect, the meaning is of wholeness. Jesus came to make people whole. He calls us to seek wholeness in our lives—a balance of spirit, mind, and body. Wholeness includes living in right relationship with others, just as we live in right relationship with God. The Bible's view on perfection is that no person is capable of living a mistake-free life. Paul wrote to the Romans, "All have sinned and fall short of the glory of God" (Rom. 3:23). It is not possible for any of us to be perfect. Even so, many people try to be perfect, only to live in near constant fear of being less than perfect.

Perfectionism is nearly always self-imposed. The perfectionist has the task of recognizing that his perfectionism is a giant that will keep him from completing many things. If you are continually striving to get something perfect, you are not likely to let it go, trust God with it, and move on to the next challenge He has for you. As a result, you can miss doing much of what the Lord wants you to do.

I have a friend who calls herself a "completionist at the A level." She strives to do her best, but once she has given her best to a job, she moves on to the next one. She gets a lot done!

In overcoming the fear of personal and professional failure, we do well to remember these words from Tom Hopkins who works with an organization called Champions Unlimited:

I never see failure as failure but only as a learning experience.

I never see failure as failure but only as the negative feedback that I need to change direction.

I never see failure as failure but only as the opportunity to develop my sense of humor.

I never see failure as failure but only as an opportunity to practice my techniques and perfect my performance.

I never see failure as failure but only as the game I must play to win.

I am not judged by the number of things that I failed but by the number of times I succeed, and the number of times I succeed is in direct proportion to the number of times that I try and may fail.

The fear of failure kept the entire army of King Saul from taking on Goliath. That same fear is at the root of perfectionism—the perfectionist frequently shies away from a challenge or opportunity out of fear that he might fail or might not be able to do his best. Such fear allows the giants to keep strutting up and down the valley, winning without ever having to put up a fight.

WHAT SCARES YOU TODAY?

What really scares you today? I mean, what causes your mouth to get dry when you think about it?

Face up to the fact that your fear stands between you and God. It may very well be the greatest giant you will ever face in your life.

Your fear may be the fear of dying or of contracting a debilitating disease.

It may be the fear of being alone or the fear that you will never have a friend.

It may be the fear of not being married or of being divorced.

It may be the fear of bankruptcy.

Or it may be the fear of losing the approval of someone important to you.

Identify your fear. If it isn't a giant in your life at this moment, it will become one. In naming your fear, you take a big step toward overcoming it.

Then go to the Lord in prayer and ask Him to give you the courage to overcome this fear and to trust Him to take care of this situation. Reach the place that Queen Esther reached when she said, "If I perish, I perish" (Est. 4:16). The great likelihood is that you won't die in doing, facing, or addressing the thing you fear most. The great likelihood is that you will stare down that giant, and he will walk away without ever even lifting his sword in your direction. James 4:7–8 gives us this encouragement: "Resist the devil and he will flee from you. Draw near to God and He will draw near to you." Call out to God in your fear, and ask Him to help you resist this enemy attack in your life. Ask Him to draw near to you.

In trusting the Lord to help you defeat your fear, you will be exercising the very faith that will carry you to victory.

CHAPTER 10

Sticking
with the
Basics

For ten years, I had the privilege of coaching high school athletes in basketball and football. During my first year of coaching, I went to Tuscaloosa, Alabama, to observe the University of Alabama's football practice under the late Coach Paul "Bear" Bryant. How excited I was as a young coach to observe the legendary coach in action!

Something he said on one of those hot summer days in August has stuck with me for the past thirty-seven years. He told his players to not forget the basics, for if you get away from the basics, you will always run into trouble. And when you do, you must go back to the basics.

Years after I quit coaching and went into school administration, that lesson remained with me, and I found it true for every area of my life. *Don't forget the basics*.

THE IMPORTANCE OF THE BASICS

If you asked the football poll experts today which team they believe is the best in high school football in America, many would no doubt name the team coached by Nick Hyder in Valdosta, Georgia. During the past decade, Hyder's teams have won more games than any other team in the nation, and they have been named national champions four times. They have won more than twenty state championships.

At the beginning of one of their practice seasons, a young aspiring coach went to Valdosta to watch Coach Hyder in action. He wanted to see what kind of practices the coach conducted, hoping to pick up a few game-winning tips.

■

Don't forget the basics.

■

He found the practices were well organized but boring to watch. They involved little more than hours of drills in blocking, tackling, throwing, catching, and kicking—the basics of football. The new coach thought to himself, *This is a lot like a Pop Warner practice—just a lot of work every day on the basics.*

At the conclusion of the week, the young coach went to Coach Hyder to thank him for the privilege of watching his practices. He said, "One thing I don't understand, Coach. You spent all of your practice time this week doing things your players should have mastered years ago. Are you in a rebuilding year?"

"No," Coach Hyder replied. "This is a veteran team. In fact, our offensive line will average more than two hundred and sixty pounds per man this season."

"Wow!" said the young coach. "Then why all the emphasis on practice in the basics?"

Coach Hyder answered, "Do you want to know the secret of my coaching success? That's why you came, isn't it? Let me tell you. The winning football teams always do the basic things the best—blocking, tackling, throwing, catching, and kicking. The more talented the athletes, the easier it is for them to get away from the basics. But it's skill in the basics that wins games."

How true! Take a look at any set of statistics for winning football teams on any given weekend in the fall, and you'll likely find that the teams with the most yards rushing, the best tackling, the best blocking, the most completed passes, and the most skillful punting statistics are the winning teams.

It's rare that a fluke play wins a game for a team that is losing statistically in a big way.

What is true in football is also true in every other sport and in every area of life. We must never lose sight of the value of the basics. If we do, we quickly slide into error, and then fear, and then the total lack of self-confidence that results in grasshopper mentality.

THE BASICS IN OUR FAMILIES

If you ask people what the basics are for a good home life, they'll probably zero in on traits such as these:

1. Spending quality time together as a family. Doing things together, including eating meals together and attending church together. Parents attending events in which their children are participating. Parents being there for their children when their children need them to be present, not only when the parents find it convenient to spend time with their children.
2. Communicating with one another. Talking over the day's activities and events, as well as the news of the neighborhood, city, nation, and world. Dealing with problems as they arise. A good home life is marked by frequent and free-flowing communication.
3. Maintaining standards related to discipline and responsibility for one another. Such discipline includes standards, chores, expressions of respect, manners, and daily regimens designed to instill order and stability into the family structure as well as to provide a "you can count on it" foundation for each family member.
4. Selfless giving, one family member to the other.

Time, communication, daily disciplines, and a giving, caring atmosphere are the hallmarks of a good home life. When we lose sight of these basics and let them slide, families begin to unravel, and eventually, the very fabric of our social structure starts to come apart.

THE BASICS OF OUR FAITH

What basics are important to faith?

You'll probably find three spiritual practices are a part of virtually every beginner's manual for those who are newly converted to Jesus Christ. These practices are mentioned frequently in tracts and booklets handed out to new believers:

1. Read your Bible every day.
2. Pray every day.
3. Attend church regularly.

The basics. We all know at some level that we should do these things. But few of us actually do them. Unfortunately, some people begin to think they are so spiritually mature that they don't need to do these things.

In the last fifty years, although more Bibles have been published and purchased than at any other time in our nation's history, we have actually seen a decline in Bible literacy. People own Bibles, but they apparently don't read them regularly or even frequently.

What do the basics do for us?

When we read our Bibles daily, we become familiar with the whole of God's Word. We see the broader context and themes of God's truth. Familiar passages that we read and reread become embedded in memory. When we know what the Bible has to say, we find it possible to apply the Bible with greater accuracy and impact to our daily problems and circumstances. The Spirit of God begins to call to our remembrance what we have planted into our minds and hearts. Also, the Word of God becomes a priority to us. In many ways, it becomes part of the way we think and respond.

We don't need to question or debate endlessly within ourselves as to whether something is right or wrong. We don't need to wonder about which course of action to take in many situations. Our moral and ethical structure is intact, and we are able to make basic decisions in keeping with the virtues of the Bible. We have a mind-set, a perspective, a way of thinking, that manifests itself in a way of living. We have values.

Much is said in our school systems about values education or value-based education. As much as our schools might do to instill values in children, we must deal with the question, Which set of values?

To know the values of the Bible, we must read and study the Bible daily.

Values don't exist in a vacuum. They aren't pulled out of thin air or isolated like molecules of hydrogen and oxygen. Values arise from a set of beliefs based upon what someone else or Someone has considered to be important.

If we don't get our value system from the Bible, where do we get it? There are few other sources, and not one of them, in my opinion, even begins to approach the supremacy of the Bible.

The values expressed in the Bible have stood the test of thousands of years of human experience. They make for an orderly, peaceful, honorable society. They give an individual a sense of purpose. They build relationships marked by fidelity, honesty, truthfulness, and generosity.

If we don't know what the Bible has to say, we are in danger of turning to weaker systems of belief for our values, which in turn have great potential for causing us to manifest arrogance, fear, doubt, anger, and pride.

To live the best quality of life, we need to base our behaviors, thoughts, words, and responses on the best quality values. And those values, in my opinion, are found in the Bible. To know the values of the Bible, we must read and study the Bible daily.

When we are in daily communication with the Lord, we find it much easier to express all of our emotions and ideas to Him. We stay emotionally and spiritually cleansed as we ask the Lord to forgive us, lead us, guide us into His paths for our lives, and provide for us. As we hear our requests and ideas being expressed before the Lord, very often we have an immediate and intuitive understanding about whether our requests are valid, our ideas are good, and our intentions and underlying motives are right. (This is especially true if we are reading our Bibles daily, too!)

■

We never outgrow our need to sleep, laugh, give and receive hugs, and exercise on a daily basis!

■

When crises hit, we don't need to become reacquainted with the One who alone is able to guide us to wise solutions or the totality of our need. We are able to come into His presence with much greater boldness as we make our requests known. We have much greater confidence that our prayer requests are in keeping with the will of heaven.

When we attend church regularly, we build Christ-centered relationships. We are in fellowship with others. We find our time priorities coming into focus as we make church attendance and participation in other church functions an important part of our schedules.

Again, when tough times come, we have a support group already in place. We don't have to build a network with others. We have one.

In an age of isolation and an eroding sense of friendship among people, regular attendance at church can become the very thing that keeps us from living lonely, isolated lives.

SPIRITUAL POWER IN THE BASICS

If you look at people you consider to be spiritually mighty or powerful today, the great likelihood is that they pray frequently, study the Bible diligently, and are in constant fellowship with other Christians. They haven't moved beyond the basics. If anything, they are spending more time on the basics than on anything else.

When a spiritual crisis hits others, they are ready spiritually to leap into action to help them. When the crisis hits their lives, they have a firm spiritual foundation and faith-filled friends.

The apostle Paul wrote about the basics of Christian behavior to the Ephesians. In the last part of his letter to them, he told wives to be in agreement with their husbands, husbands to love their wives, children to obey their parents, parents to bring up their children in the training and admonition of the Lord, servants to obey their masters as if they were obeying Christ, masters to treat their servants as they would want Christ to treat them, and all the people in the church to be "strong in the Lord." (See Eph. 5:17–6:10.)

Paul reminded them of the basics of a Christ-centered relationship—even though the church was large, well established, and known for its spiritual power and influence all over Asia Minor.

Paul went on to describe how they could stay strong in the Lord. He told them to put on the whole armor of God— giant-slaying armor. The armor was spiritual in nature and it involved these elements:

- Truth
- Righteousness
- The gospel of peace
- Faith
- Salvation
- The Word of God

Again, we see the basics! And what were the Ephesians to do once they were fully armed for spiritual battle? They were to pray and be on continual alert against evil, and to stand with perseverance and boldness. Yet again, the basics. (See Eph. 6:13–19.)

The church of Ephesus was known for its great teaching influence, its works of righteousness, its diligent and persevering labor, its patience with new converts, its ability to test apostles to see if they were of God. Even so, the apostle John relays these words of Christ to this church in the book of

Revelation: "You have left your first love. . . . Repent and do the first works" (2:4–5). The Ephesians are called to return to *the basics!*

THE VALUE OF BASICS IN TIMES OF CRISIS

We never outgrow our need for reading God's Word, praying, and being intimately involved with a church body. In fact, our need for these basics increases as we grow spiritually.

Consider the basic needs of the human body. As infants, we required food. As adults, we require fewer feedings, but even more food. And we still require food on a daily basis.

As infants, we required liquids. As adults, we need to drink even more water. And again, on a daily basis.

We never outgrow our need to sleep, laugh, give and receive hugs, and exercise on a daily basis!

In times of stress or illness, what do we do? We return to the basics—good nutrition, sufficient rest, and lots of fluids.

The same principle holds for our spiritual lives. The busier our schedules, the more pressure we feel, the bigger the giants we face, the more we are struggling to overcome grasshopper mentality, the more important it is that we stick with the basics vital to our faith, our families, and our work.

Three young men knew that to be true as they faced a giant of a ruler and a giant of a problem. Hananiah, Mishael, and Azariah had been carted hundreds of miles away from their homeland by an enemy king. They had little hope of returning to their native land. Even their own prophets said that their captivity was a consequence of spiritual disobedience of God.

In their new home of Babylon they were subjected to various techniques and practices aimed at stripping away their previous identities and instilling in them the grasshopper mentality of servants and slaves. They were taught a new language, told new religious stories, given different food and beverages, and compelled to learn new skills. They were also given new names, ones we tend to use today in describing them: Shadrach, Meshach, and Abed-Nego.

One day the three men faced a giant in the form of the king they had been trained to serve. His name was Nebuchadnezzar. The king had built a giant statue of himself out of gold, and at the suggestion of his subordinates, he required all the people to bow down and worship the statue when a certain musical signal was given.

Put yourself into the position of the three young men for a moment. You are far from home. Everything that was familiar to you has been stripped away. You have been trained in a systematic way to serve a powerful emperor, and now you are told that when you hear a certain sound, you are to bow down on cue. You are told that if you exercise your will and fail to worship this golden statue, you will be thrown into a fiery furnace.

Everything about your life has the markings of grasshopper mentality. But deep inside the spirit of the three young men was giant-slaying thinking. As much as the outward trappings and identity of their lives had been changed, they still knew the commandments of God, and they still feared God more than man.

What did they do in the face of their giant?

They got back down to the basics. When Nebuchadnezzar confronted them about their rebellion and asked them, "Who is the god who will deliver you from my hands?" they responded by saying, in essence, "We don't even need to pause to consider the answer to that question." And then they said, "Our God whom we serve is able to deliver us from the burning fiery furnace, and He will deliver us from your hand."

What a bold statement of faith!

And then they said, "But if not, let it be known to you, O king, that we do not serve your gods, nor will we worship the gold image which you have set up." (See Dan. 3:1–18.)

Hananiah, Mishael, and Azariah knew God could deliver them. They believed God *would* deliver them. But they also believed that even if God chose not to deliver them, they were better off standing tall as giant slayers and trusting God with their lives than worshiping a false image that God had told them never to worship.

Hananiah, Mishael, and Azariah didn't have time to go back and learn the basics in that crisis moment. They didn't have time to learn the commandments of God or search the Scriptures or enter into a discussion about what was right or wrong. The basics of their trust in God and their knowledge of God's laws were already deeply implanted in them—so deeply ingrained in their spirits that no matter what the Chaldeans did to them to try to brainwash them into a new way of thinking and acting, they could stand firm in a moment of decision and crisis.

We all know how the story turned out. Nebuchadnezzar had the three young men thrown into the fiery furnace, but they did not die there. Instead, a "fourth man" appeared in the furnace with them. In Nebuchadnezzar's own words, the fourth man looked like the Son of God.

Nebuchadnezzar had the men pulled from the furnace. When he saw that not a hair of their heads was singed, their garments remained unscorched, and they didn't even smell like fire, he declared,

> Blessed be the God of Shadrach, Meshach, and Abed-Nego, who sent His Angel and delivered His servants who trusted in Him, and they have frustrated the king's word, and yielded their bodies, that they should not serve nor worship any god except their own God! Therefore I make a decree that any people, nation, or language which speaks anything amiss against the God of Shadrach, Meshach, and Abed-Nego shall be cut in pieces, and their houses shall be made an ash heap; because there is no other God who can deliver like this.

Not only did Hananiah, Mishael, and Azariah win spiritual freedom for all the Jewish people in captivity, they were promoted in the king's service! (See Dan. 3:26–30.)

The simple truth is this: *when the basics are in place, crises can be faced.*

STRAYING FROM BASICS IS DANGEROUS

A coach knows that a player is courting disaster when he begins to rely on his athletic prowess to the neglect of the basics.

A businessman begins to run into danger when he starts trusting his instincts and throws all standard financial principles aside.

A husband or wife flirts with disaster when he or she takes a marriage for granted and stops doing the basics related to romance, appreciation, and expressions of love.

Parents put themselves into the danger zone when they stop disciplining their children, spending time with them, communicating openly with them, or making them a priority.

And in our spiritual lives, we are opening ourselves up to evil itself when we say,

"I'm too busy today to read God's Word. I'll do it tomorrow."

"I don't have time today to pray. God will understand."

"It's all right if I don't go to church this Sunday. I don't need to go every Sunday. I can miss a time or two."

Stick to the basics. Stay after them. Immerse yourself in them. They are the keys to building up all of the inner resources necessary to acquire and maintain a giant-slaying mind-set.

CHAPTER 11

Focusing Like a Fox

My friend and former secretary, Estelle Hill, no longer operates the one-hundred-acre farm that she and her young son inherited after her husband died. Through the years, however, she told me many of the lessons she learned during her busy, sometimes uncertain, but fruitful years as a farmer. One of the lessons involved an old gray fox who lived in the woods next to their pasture.

In the quiet predawn light, when the woodlands bordering the pasture were still wrapped in darkness, that old gray fox would lie in wait for the chickens to leave their roosts and make their way into the pasture. There, they would begin feeding on the tender shoots of the grain that had been planted specifically for them, clucking their hushed little "t-uuuuck, tuck, tuck" sounds as they fed.

Once they were in the center of the pasture, that old fox would come streaking from the woods like a bolt of lightning, his eyes glued on one particular chicken. In pursuit of that chicken, he would run into and even leap over other chickens, often sending feathers flying in all directions. No matter how many other chickens might be between him and his targeted prey, he never took his eye off the one chicken he had chosen to be his breakfast.

There was little the chickens or Estelle could do. There was no way to counter the fox's attack since he moved so swiftly. Once back in the woods with his prey, there was little use in tracking him since he blended into the clumps of branches, and he was too canny ever to enter the pasture from the same spot two times in a row.

Eventually, the fox died, but Estelle will wager that he did not starve to death!

Estelle credits that old fox with teaching her about the value of sticking to a goal. When she was presented with an opportunity to go into beef cattle production, she weighed the option carefully. Her goal, however, was to operate a completely diversified farm and to remain debt free. To go into cattle, she would have had to put a mortgage on the farm to finance the purchase of breeding stock. She decided to remain focused on what she knew she could handle.

A few years after that opportunity was presented to her, the cattle market plunged, and big farmers in her area lost heavily, a number of them going into bankruptcy. Estelle, however, remained solvent. She and her fourteen-year-old son became the only woman and child in the state of South Carolina ever to earn the "Balanced Farm Award" given in recognition of excellence in farming.

■ *Focus on one problem.* ■

Hunters have learned from watching animals stalk and capture their prey. Bird hunters, for example, know that when they flush a covey of quail from a field, they will be most successful if they pick out one bird and shoot directly and solely at it. The temptation, of course, is to shoot at the entire covey, but the successful way is to shoot at one bird at a time.

DEVELOPING A SINGULAR EYE

The tendency of those who suffer from grasshopper mentality is to see masses of giants. If we look closely at what the spies said when they returned from Canaan, we find a broad generalization: "All the people whom we saw in it are men of great stature. There we saw the giants" (Num. 13:32–33).

No mention is made of a singular or individual giant. There is no description of one person, no name, no specific location. Rather, all the people are giants, and apparently, all the people are men, too!

■ *Take each day as it comes.* ■ Any time we focus on generalities, stereotypes, and masses, we are likely to be overwhelmed and sink into grasshopper mentality. Teachers and parents of teenagers hear such generalizations all the time:

"Everybody gets to go, except me."

"All the kids have this."

"Nobody else has to do this."

All the other girls are pretty, and all the other guys are handsome. All the other parents are understanding. All the other kids are smart. The fact is that if a child is forced to focus on just one peer at a time, the story often is dramatically different.

The person with grasshopper mentality nearly always compares himself to groups of people, struggles with what he perceives to be deep character flaws that cloud any issue or opportunity, and sees things in terms of always and never, all or none.

In becoming a winner in the land of giants, you need to focus on one problem, pursue one goal, work on one character trait, and take each day as it comes. Focus is vital if you are to hit a giant right between the eyes.

LEAVE THE REST OF THE
PHILISTINES TO SAUL

Not only can our goals fade away into fuzziness, but sometimes we can have cloudy vision in seeing our enemies.

Focus on one problem at a time. Don't try to change everything that is wrong at once. Dissect your problem into manageable pieces, and take on the most important aspect of the problem first. Then move to the next most important part of the problem. And so forth. Pretty soon you will have dealt with the entire mess.

When David faced the entire army of the Philistines, he saw only one man. He didn't fight the Philistines per se. He fought Goliath. David wisely left the rest of the Philistines to the other men in Saul's army.

Have you ever stopped to think about what it means for something to become a plague? A plague can be anything that afflicts or troubles a person. It can be a deadly epidemic disease or a nuisance.

Our problems—our giants—sometimes seem to come at us in plague proportions. We feel overwhelmed by them. They seem like locusts swarming overhead or like frogs jumping into everything from cooking pots to beds. They seem like stinging gnats we can never seem to kill or like hail that can't be escaped. Plagues overwhelm us to a great extent by their volume.

Problems that strike us as individuals, however, rarely come in plague proportion. Think back to the plagues that came as the result of Pharaoh refusing to let the children of Israel leave Egypt as God had commanded. All of the plagues except the last came upon the "land" of Egypt. The only problem that struck at individual lives was the plague of death to the firstborn. And for that plague, the Lord gave a very specific set of instructions so the Israelites would not have to experience it. Each family was to deal with the coming problem by applying the blood of a lamb to the doorway of the home and then eating the lamb that had been slain in a prescribed manner. Those who followed God's commandments were spared.

When you are facing what seems to be an onslaught of problems—a plague of problems—regain your focus. Don't let the swarm blind you.

Identify the problem that hits your life in a specific way.

Your company may be in turmoil. Isolate the one aspect of the turmoil that may affect your life and yours alone.

Your city may be rocking and reeling in the wake of a violent riot or perhaps an earthquake. Isolate the damage or potential damage to your life.

Your life may seem to be turned upside down by the death of a loved one. Focus on what you still have in your life and what you must do to regain your balance in the wake of your loss.

Zero in on the problem. And then, go to the Lord. He has provided a way for you to walk through this problem and emerge victorious. Go to His Word. Look for the commandments and promises of God that relate directly to your particular situation. Ask God to reveal to you what you must do specifically and immediately. The Word of God applies to you if you will only apply it!

The key is to focus. And then to persist.

FOCUSING ON GOALS AND PLANS

The ability to set goals is one trait that sets people apart from all other creatures. A goal is different from a dream. A dream is a picture of the world the way we want it to be or as it should be. A goal is a picture of the world the way we are willing to work to make it become.

You might dream, for example, of living in a city where there are no homeless people and everybody has a decent dinner every night of the year. That's only a dream, however, unless you decide to do something about homeless and hungry people. Having a goal of ridding your city of homelessness and hunger will likely involve other people, and to reach your goal, you will need to develop a plan. Plans state specifically what is going to be done, by whom, in what time frame, at what cost (in terms of both time and resources). Most plans are linked to identifiable outcomes that can be defined and measured. Ultimately, a realistic plan turns a goal into a realized dream.

The path from dream to development of a plan requires commitment. Commitment is a belief in yourself and the worthiness of your effort. In many ways, commitment is obedience to the plan. It is staying dedicated to the thing that you want to accomplish, and doing everything within your power to marshal your resources toward a positive result.

JOSHUA WAS A FOCUSED LEADER

Joshua had a dream of living in the Promised Land. He was one of the two spies who had returned from Canaan with a positive report. For forty years of wandering through the wilderness, Joshua kept the dream alive that he might one day live in the land flowing with milk and honey, a land he described as "exceedingly good."

■ *The path from dream to plan requires commitment.* ■

The day came when the Lord asked Joshua to stop dreaming and start acting. The dream was about to be turned into a goal. In the book of Joshua, we read how the Lord came to Joshua after the death of Moses and said,

> Arise, go over this Jordan, you and all this people, to the land which I am giving to them—the children of Israel. Every place that the sole of your foot will tread upon I have given you. . . . Be strong and of good courage, for to this people you shall divide as an inheritance the land which I swore to their fathers to give them. . . . Observe to do according to all the law which Moses My servant commanded you (Josh. 1:2–7).

Notice that the goal was stated in far more specific terms than the dream: "go over this Jordan," "every place that the sole of your foot will tread upon," "you shall divide as an inheritance the land," "observe to do according to all the law."

Joshua knew that to realize the dream, he had to mobilize the people to cross, walk, and divide the land, keeping the law of Moses as they went.

Three times, the Lord said to Joshua, "Be strong and of

good courage." The Lord knew that for the goal to be reached, Joshua was going to have to stay committed and keep his faith focused.

The goal was then turned into a plan. Joshua commanded the people to "prepare provisions." He told which people were to remain east of the Jordan. He sent two men to spy out the land, especially Jericho.

What happened on the spying mission?

We see a reversal of grasshopper mentality! The two spies went into the city and found refuge in the house of Rahab. She said to them,

> I know that the LORD has given you the land, that the terror of you has fallen on us, and that all the inhabitants of the land are fainthearted because of you. For we have heard how the LORD dried up the water of the Red Sea for you when you came out of Egypt, and what you did to the two kings of the Amorites who were on the other side of the Jordan. . . . And as soon as we heard these things, our hearts melted; neither did there remain any more courage in anyone because of you, for the LORD your God, He is God in heaven above and on earth beneath (Josh. 2:9–11).

After asking the spies to spare her and her family when they conquered Jericho, Rahab helped them escape.

When the two spies returned, they spoke giant-slaying words, not words rooted in grasshopper mentality. They said to Joshua, "Truly the LORD has delivered all the land into our hands, for indeed all the inhabitants of the country are fainthearted because of us" (Josh. 2:24).

Don't let any obstacle stand in your way.

Joshua led the people across the Jordan, and on the other side, the Lord gave Joshua the rest of His plan for conquering Jericho. The priests and the armed men were to go in procession around the walls of Jericho once a day for six days—armed men, trumpeters, priests bearing the ark of the covenant, and the rear guard all marching in silence except for the priests blowing the trumpets of rams' horns. On the seventh day, they were to march around the city seven times, then the trumpets were to be blown, and the people were to shout.

The Lord had given Joshua a very specific plan. And for seven days they carried it out in detail—staying focused on the plan and staying committed to accomplishing it.

On the seventh day, as the trumpets blared and the people shouted, "the wall fell down flat" (Josh. 6:20). The people rushed into the city and utterly destroyed all that was in it except for Rahab and her family.

It took many more years, and many more battles, before Joshua had subdued all of the cities and territories that the Lord led him to conquer. All those years, Joshua was living in a dream fulfilled—he was living in the land flowing with milk and honey, an exceedingly good land. He had to work in that land, of course. He had to fight battles and conquer enemies. But his focus on his dream, then his goal, and then his plan paid off.

DON'T LET OBSTACLES
CLOUD YOUR FOCUS

Do you think you are too old to set a new goal or make a new plan in your life? Grandma Moses didn't think so, and she became well known for the paintings she produced in the later years of her life. Colonel Sanders didn't think so, and he founded a chain of restaurants that specialized in Kentucky-fried chicken.

Do you think your nationality keeps you from making a certain goal or plan? Virtually every immigrant to our nation managed to overcome this obstacle!

Is your religion something you perceive as being a stumbling block to your focused commitment to a goal or plan? John F. Kennedy overcame the fact that no Catholic had been elected to the presidency. Gandhi changed the nation of India by using some of the techniques associated with his religion.

What about race? Is your race being blamed for your lack

of focus on a goal or your commitment to a plan? Nelson Mandela leads South Africa today. Martin Luther King, Jr., changed the way people regarded civil rights of blacks. You need only look around to see how many nonwhites hold high public office and have reached the top of the business, entertainment, and athletic worlds in recent decades.

Do you consider your sex to be an obstacle? Women are breaking into what were once male-only fields of employment by the droves.

Don't let any obstacle stand in your way and keep you from pursuing the dream God has planted in your heart. Don't let the actions of others keep you from doing your best, giving your utmost, and going to the top.

One of my favorite poems is about focusing ourselves on the highest and best life has to offer—in spite of what others may do.

Give Your Best

People are unreasonable, illogical and self-centered. Love them anyway.
If you do good, people will accuse you of selfish, ulterior motives. Do good anyway.
If you are successful, you will win false friends and true enemies. Succeed anyway.
Honesty and frankness make you vulnerable. Be honest and frank anyway.
The good you do today will be forgotten tomorrow.
Do good anyway.
The biggest people with the biggest ideas can be shot down by the smallest people with the smallest minds. Think big anyway.
People favor underdogs but follow only top dogs.
Fight for some underdogs anyway.
What you spend years building may be destroyed overnight.
Build anyway.
Give the world the best you have and you'll get kicked in the teeth. Give the world the best you've got anyway. (Author unknown)

Stay focused. Do what you know to do, are called to do, and believe is right to do. Stay focused and persist, no matter what others do.

GO IN THE DIRECTION YOU'RE HEADED—UNTIL YOU ARRIVE!

In the movie *Forrest Gump,* the one outstanding trait that Gump seems to have is his ability to focus. He runs with all his might in whatever direction he is aimed—ideally toward the goal line! He focuses on a Ping-Pong ball with diligence and becomes a world champion. He focuses on getting men away from enemy fire in Vietnam until he collapses in exhaustion. He focuses on shrimping until the day comes when he is in the right place at the right time. He focuses his love on one girl until he wins her heart. Gump isn't bright. He is lucky. But mostly, he is a one-direction kind of guy. He goes in whatever direction he is aimed, full speed ahead.

One of the great heroes in the Bible was a man who never seemed to lose his focus: Joseph. Joseph had dreams as a young man—dreams he perhaps unwisely shared with others. The two dreams confirmed the same truth: God had a plan for his life, and it was a plan that called him to become a leader, a one-in-a-million somebody. He never lost sight of that dream or stopped believing in the God who gave it to him.

Joseph was sold into slavery by his brothers, but he didn't lose his personal focus.

Joseph was betrayed by his boss's wife and cast into a dungeon, but he didn't lose his focus.

Joseph was overlooked by a person he befriended and encouraged, but he didn't lose his focus.

Joseph emerged a victor and drew this conclusion about all his past troubles after he was reunited with his family: "God sent me before you to preserve life" (Gen. 45:5).

Is there a dream that God has put in your heart today? Focus on it. Crystallize it into goals. Pursue it with a plan. Stay focused on it. And persist.

CHAPTER 12

Standing
Up to
Intimidation

W ho intimidates you?
Nearly everyone I've met is or has been intimidated by someone. Stop and think about it for a few moments.

Which people do you feel uncomfortable around, or perhaps more important, who do you perceive wishes *you* weren't around?

Who causes your palms to grow clammy, your heart to pound, your stomach to ball up into a knot, and your brow to break out into a cold sweat?

Among all the people you know, which ones do you feel would be least likely to pay you a compliment or perhaps even to acknowledge your presence?

Which people do you feel are so powerful or so great that you would not be worthy so much as to hold the door open for them?

For some people, the intimidating person might be one of the following:

- Physician
- Dentist
- Lawyer
- Judge

- Law enforcement officer
- Teacher
- Principal
- Member of the armed forces
- Business executive
- Preacher
- Anybody who seems to be the boss

No one class of person or holder of a particular job position is necessarily intimidating. A person becomes intimidating only because another person allows himself to become intimidated.

Sometimes your intimidators are people that others might think would never intimidate you at all.

I received a letter from a school principal in West Virginia. He wrote that he had heard me speak during the previous year, and as a result, he had become determined to develop his own self-confidence and overcome the inferiority complex that had plagued him for years. He stated that competent teachers had always been threatening to him, but that he was now feeling much more secure and sure of himself in their presence.

I suspect that many people we think of as leaders are actually intimidated by those who work for them, serve under them, and even look up to them. Managers are often intimidated by up-and-coming employees whom they perceive to be only temporarily beneath them on the corporate ladder. Pastors are frequently intimidated by members of their congregations. I heard about an anesthesiologist who chose that particular medical specialty because he was scared to death of patients. He preferred to deal primarily with people who were under anesthesia and couldn't talk back or ask questions!

Ask yourself, Is there someone I know who seems always to come out the winner, no matter what either one of us does or says? Who do I believe holds me in contempt and considers me unworthy of notice? That is the person or those are the people who intimidate you.

INTIMIDATORS VARY WIDELY

For some people, the intimidator bears a badge of authority. That was the case for Marge. She had suffered an assault of verbal abuse from a security guard when she was only three years old, and to this day, she cringes at the sight of anyone wearing a badge.

For some, the intimidator is an individual—a parent or other relative, a teacher, a neighbor—someone who has exerted power over them in the past and who is perceived to cause emotional or physical harm. That is the situation for Bob, who can't bear to be in the presence of his father. When Dad walks into a room, Bob walks out. He firmly believes that no matter what he says or does, Dad will have a better idea, a wittier response, or a more dominant opinion.

For some, the intimidator is a class of people. Sam was intimidated by anyone living in a house. You see, Sam was born into poverty, and for the first eighteen years of his life, he lived in small, dark, cramped apartments. One day as a seven-year-old boy, Sam rode the bus with his mother, and as they passed through a fine residential area, Sam asked about the buildings that lined the streets. His mother replied, "Those are the homes where the rich people live."

"How many people live in one of those buildings?" Sam asked.

"Oh, just one family," his mother answered. From that day on, Sam felt intimidated by anyone who could afford to have a house.

In John's case, the intimidation relates to all men who are taller than he, especially in business settings. Since John stands only five feet three inches tall, he has a lot of intimidators! It doesn't seem to matter that John is the founder and CEO of a successful manufacturing plant. He still dreads stand-up meetings with his clients, vendors, and colleagues.

In Jo Ellen's case, the class of intimidators included all who had finished college. She had dropped out after her freshman year, and she found it difficult to feel good about holding her own in a conversation with anyone who had completed a degree. Jo Ellen had a tendency to assume that others had degrees, even when they didn't. She expected to be intimidated.

Each of these people suffered from grasshopper mentality.

THE NATURE OF INTIMIDATORS

What does this word *intimidate* really mean? It means to "make timid—to fill with fear, to overawe, to deter by discouraging." Intimidation causes people to cower, to struggle against something they suspect is bigger and more powerful than they are.

Intimidators who consciously and purposefully intend to intimidate others nearly always emphasize one or more of these elements:

- Control
- Competition
- Winning
- Power

■

Encouragers look for win-win situations.

■

Competition sometimes comes in the form of comparison. People who intimidate us are likely to be people we believe to be continually comparing us to themselves or to others. Our fear is that we won't measure up.

Few people thrive in an environment or a relationship in which winning and power are emphasized constantly. On the other hand, most people are comfortable and relaxed in environments and relationships marked by these qualities:

- Cooperation
- Mutual satisfaction
- Joint decision making

These are the hallmarks of people I call encouragers. Encouragers look for win-win situations rather than one-winner-takes-all situations. Encouragers seek cooperation rather than competition. Encouragers respect and value others instead of putting them down. Encouragers are not necessarily weak, emotional, or indecisive people. On the contrary, they are often very strong and effective leaders, with bold ideas and creative solutions—gained in part through their ability to interact with others. Encouragers are far more popular than intimidators, a factor that tends to benefit them greatly because people open up to them and give them ideas and suggestions that they can use to help others.

We must stand up!

What then can you do to enhance your ability to become a winner in the land of giants?

First, choose to associate with encouragers. Marry an encourager, attend a church led by an encourager, work for an encourager, and hire encouragers.

Second, refuse to compete or play the compare game with an intimidator. Suggest cooperation to the person privately, and if the person refuses that option, suggest cooperation to the person in the presence of a third party who is willing to cooperate.

Third, turn your eyes away from the intimidator and find someone that you might encourage. A number of psychologists advise their depressed clients to make someone else feel good as a part of their therapy. When you encourage someone else to believe that he or she is a giant slayer, you reinforce your own giant-slaying thinking!

STANDING UP TO INTIMIDATORS

What must we do when we come face-to-face with people who intimidate us?

We must stand up!

A number of times in my life I have had to stand up to people who attempted to intimidate me.

One of the first was when I was a young teacher and two African American teenagers—Patricia and Josephine—came to our white high school. It was the first time in the history of Alabama that two African American youths attempted to attend a white school.

People everywhere were talking about boycotting the school and picketing. Some people were driving around the school, urging people to leave the school. The school was eventually surrounded by National Guardsmen with machine guns!

One afternoon, a couple of men broke into the back of the school and began running through the halls urging everybody to walk out and to make the boycott truly successful.

I refused to budge. I said, "Listen, my job is to teach, not to make some kind of political statement. I'm not going to leave my job. My job is not to decide *who* I teach. My job is to teach."

I was born in the South and grew up in the South. Nobody could seem to understand why I felt the way I did. My family and I were warned to sleep at the back of the house in case somebody threw rocks through the windows at the front of the house.

The situation remained tense until the day when a church in the Birmingham area was bombed and four African American youths were killed. It took their deaths, it seemed, for people to see how vile their hatred had become.

My stance, of course, was nothing compared to that taken by those young girls, who had molasses and flour thrown on them and were called all kinds of names.

That was the first time I ever felt exposed to such intense pressure for doing what I knew to be right. And I learned a key principle in that regarding our standing up to intimidation: *we need to be sure that what we are standing for is what Jesus Christ stood for.*

If we stand in self-pride, we'll fall.

If we stand for something that is evil, the Lord will topple us over.

If we stand for something that is right, the Lord stands with us, and we stand in certainty and strength.

That doesn't automatically mean we won't have to pay a price. We may be persecuted. The giant before us may bellow at us or even get in a blow or two.

That was the case for Dave Williams. A tackle for the Houston Oilers, Dave missed a game a few seasons back because he chose to stay with his wife as she gave birth to their son Scott. The team fined him $110,000 for missing the game.

On a nationally televised show, program host Connie Chung asked him about paying $110,000 to be with his wife in the delivery room. Williams said, "There isn't enough money in the world to trade for that moment. Family comes first." Chung asked him, "If the fine had been for a million dollars, would you have still missed the game?" He said, "Yes."

Dave Williams may have lost some money, but he retained his principles. Thomas Jefferson once said, "In matters of taste, swim in the current; in matters of principle, stand like a rock." Dave Williams stood like a rock. He did what was right. And in the end, that type of behavior results in victory.

There are other times when the cost is dearer than money.

In Acts 6–7, we read how Stephen, "full of faith and power," stood up to those who accused him in the highest court of his faith of being a blasphemer. Stephen addressed his accusers in such a way that they "saw his face as the face of an angel." Stephen spoke with boldness and an assurance that comes when we know we are speaking what God would have us to say.

Stephen was stoned to death by those who attempted to intimidate him. The fact was, the intimidators became the intimidated. Stephen's accusers were intimidated by the truth that Stephen preached to them.

You may say, "Well, that sounds like defeat to me."

Stephen and all those in the early church didn't see it that way. They saw it as a great victory.

Did Jesus stand up for Stephen? He certainly did! Shortly before Stephen was stoned, he had a vision of heaven, in which he saw the glory of God and Jesus standing at the right hand of God. He cried out, "Look! I see the heavens opened and the Son of Man standing at the right hand of God!" (Acts 7:56).

Elsewhere in the New Testament we read that when Jesus ascended into heaven, He was seated at the right hand of the Father. But for Stephen, Jesus stood up. In my mind's eye I see Him cheering for Stephen, then reaching out His hand to him to welcome him home to heaven. Yes, Jesus stood for Stephen. And in the end, Stephen's actions were recorded for all time. He earned a place in the New Testament and a place in the history of the church that can never be taken away.

When we stand for right, the Lord stands with us—both on earth and in heaven, both now and for all eternity.

REFUSING TO TRADE EASE FOR WRONG

I learned a second great principle about standing up to intimidation when I was a superintendent of schools.

In my school district, an African American principal led a predominantly white school. Nine parents decided that they wanted that principal fired. They leveled some of the most heinous and ridiculous charges against the man. We had him fully investigated and found that each of the charges made against him was false. At the core of the charges and their hatred, of course, was racism. The parents didn't want the man as the principal of their children's school solely because he was African American.

Never compromise your belief in what is right.

A number of people suggested to me that I put the man in a different position. Their arguments were nearly always couched in these terms: "This will be better for everybody. The parents will be appeased. He won't have to put up with pressure. The community won't be polarized. He can get on with the business of being an excellent principal elsewhere."

I said, "I won't do it. He has an outstanding record, and he hasn't done anything wrong. I won't let nine parents run this man off or smudge his career."

Before I knew it, members of the Black Caucus and the NAACP were involved. African Americans and whites were verbalizing strong opinions.

The majority of the leaders in the town and the newspaper had their children in private schools. Untruths were published, and in many ways, the reporting and the editorializing were slanted in favor of the white parents against the African American principal. An African American minister in the city asked me to go with him to the newspaper to talk with the publisher-owner of the paper.

I agreed to go. At the newspaper offices, I said to the owner, "I'm going to do what is right. The man has not done anything inappropriate. Not one of the charges against him has been proved to be true. He is a victim in this situation. Why should a man's career be destroyed because of the false allegations of nine people?"

Several people said to me, "Listen, this is getting too hot, and the heat is continuing to build. It's stupid for you to take the heat for this man. If you continue to stand up for him, they'll soon be going after you, too." A few people took me to lunch or out for drives to explain to me how vicious the opposition might get or what might happen to me or my family.

By law in that district, a school board couldn't fire a principal unless the superintendent of schools recommended his dismissal. I refused to give that recommendation or to reassign him.

The most profession-related anguish and pain that we ever went through as a family occurred during that time. Standing up to intimidators can be agonizing. But the principle came through clearly to me: *there is no win in a compromising of values.*

Lots of things can be compromised—differences regarding

methods, schedules, priorities, style, location. But if you compromise your values to gain a temporary victory for yourself, you lose in the long run. One of the main things you lose is your integrity. And right behind it are your courage and your faith.

We must never compromise our belief in what is right, especially when we have a deep heartfelt assurance that it is right in God's sight and according to God's Word. Of course, we must not be pigheaded about our beliefs. We must *know* with certainty that what we believe is in God's Word and that we understand God's Word in the full context of its meaning.

I had absolute certainty in my heart that the man was being treated unfairly. God's Word tells us that God is no respecter of persons when it comes to justice. African American people and white people deserve the same fairness under our laws and certainly under God's law. God's Word tells us to uphold the innocent and to stand for the person who is wrongfully accused. That was the case with the principal.

We investigated the man's behavior and record because we wanted to make certain that he hadn't made an error. In so doing, we were following God's Word to judge a situation and to search for wrongdoing. If we had found mistakes, we certainly would have brought them to light and taken action but, again, regardless of the man's race.

If we are going to stand up to intimidators, we need to make certain that we have right on our side. In that, we will have the Lord on our side. We may be persecuted in the process, but we will not fail.

GOD PROVIDES A WAY OF ESCAPE

In certain instances, God provides a way of escape after we have stood up to those intimidating us. At times, the way of escape appears after we have made our final resolve and before we are required to make a public stand.

The apostle Paul certainly knew that to be true in his life. Time and again, Paul was smuggled out of town under the cloak of darkness. Once he was let over a city wall in a basket. He left Ephesus shortly after a near riot in the great theater. Yet Paul never left town with his tail between his legs. He left not in defeat but in victory.

Why is that so? Because Paul never compromised his beliefs or refused to stand for the gospel of Christ. He was tortured, imprisoned, and nearly killed on a number of occasions in standing up to those who opposed him. At other times, his victory came through an escape so that he might live and preach yet another day in another place.

My family and I experienced this in our lives as the issue regarding the African American principal began to cool some. I was offered a larger and better-paying position in Maryland. About that same time, Mrs. Norman Vincent Peale said in a telephone conversation to me, "Billy, the Lord never shuts a small door but that He opens up a larger one." Her comments had nothing to do about the situation I was facing in the district, but I took them as a word from the Lord that I was to move through the larger door that the Lord was opening for me.

God had provided a way for us to escape further persecution, without compromising our values. Matthew 5:10 tells us, "Happy are those who are persecuted because they are good, for the Kingdom of Heaven is theirs" (TLB). We saw the position in Maryland as the reward God had for our standing strong despite persecution.

At times you will need to stand up to intimidation. Stand strong when you know you are right, and refuse to compromise the values you know to be embedded in truth. God will stand with you and enable you to endure the persecution you receive, or He will provide a way for you to escape and continue to stand strong in a new place.

We do the standing. Handling our intimidators is His business.

CHAPTER 13

The High Cost of Carelessness

B ack in 1967, when I was the principal of a junior high school in Huntsville, Alabama, I was asked to speak at a PTA meeting one evening. In anticipation of that event, I decided to have my hair trimmed. As soon as the school day ended, I jumped into my VW and raced to the barbershop to keep a 3:30 P.M. appointment. Entering the shop, I took off my coat and was greeted by the owner and shown to a chair.

In those days, a razor cut was the thing. Before each haircut, a barber generally sharpened his razor by pulling it back and forth across a razor strap that was held perpendicular to the chair.

The barber and a couple of other men in the shop and I began to talk about football as I sat down in the chair. I put my arms on the armrests and let each hand extend over the end of the armrest in a fairly relaxed manner. The barber pulled out the razor strap, only he pulled it out parallel to the armrest. As he began to swipe the razor back and forth across the strap, suddenly the razor hit the middle finger on my right hand and I looked down to see the bottom half of my finger lying on the floor!

I jumped from the chair and ran to the sink. I grabbed a

white towel and wrapped it around my hand as I put it under the cold water faucet. I then asked the barber to call the Huntsville Hospital and get Dr. C. P. Cotter on the line. Cradling the phone receiver between my chin and my ear, I told the doctor what had happened. He asked me if I could get to the hospital, and I told him I could. My finger was surgically repaired at the hospital, and I went back to school and made the PTA presentation. (The finger healed beautifully. Even my fingernail grew back.)

Carelessness costs.
■ ■

Later that evening, I had a call from the barber. He was concerned that I was going to sue him. He told me that a lawsuit would ruin his business and destroy his ability to provide for his family. I assured him that I had no plan to sue him, and I reassured him that I was all right.

He said, "Mr. Mitchell, that was plain carelessness on my part. You never swipe a razor without pulling the strap out away from the chair. Those few seconds of carelessness nearly cost you the end of your finger, and could have cost me my business. Thank you for not suing me. I want you to know that I've learned a big lesson out of this—carelessness costs."

The cost of carelessness is sometimes quite high. I learned that in a slightly different way while mowing my lawn one day. That time, I was the one who was careless rather than the victim of someone else's momentary lapse.

BE SURE TO CHECK THE DETAILS

I have always enjoyed cutting grass and working in the yard. When I was a boy, I cut lawns for twenty-five cents. To me, that was big money.

When we bought a house with a one-acre lawn, I wasn't the least bit daunted by the idea of mowing such a large lawn. I was eager to meet the challenge.

Knowing how I enjoyed yard work, but also wanting to see some of my weekend time devoted to other activities, my wife bought me a riding lawn mower as a Christmas present.

Almost every time I went out to cut the grass, my wife would say, "Billy, did you check the oil and gas?" I'm not quite sure why she was more concerned about those details than I was. Perhaps it was because I remembered the days of being the energy behind a push mower that didn't require either. Sometimes I checked the oil and gas, but I must admit, much of the time I did not. I filled the tank with gasoline when I ran out, and I rarely, if ever, checked the oil level.

Thirteen months after I had taken possession of my riding lawn mower, and after I had been running at full throttle for about an hour one afternoon, I suddenly heard a loud "Pow! Pow!" The mower came to a stop. I knew intuitively that I was in big trouble.

Reluctantly, I told Carolyn what had happened. Then I called a friend, and he came over and put the lawn mower in his truck. We took it back to the shop where Carolyn purchased it. The proprietor took one quick look and informed me that I had blown the engine; there wasn't a drop of oil in the engine. Because there was no oil, the warranty would not cover the problem. It wouldn't have mattered, actually, since the warranty had expired the month before. The fee for my carelessness? Three hundred and fifty dollars, plus a hundred dollars to have the yard mowed twice while the mower was in the shop.

Today, I check the oil each time before I use a lawn mower.

In the case of my incident at the barbershop, I was the victim of a one-time instance of carelessness. In the case of my damaged lawn mower, I was the perpetrator of a pattern of carelessness. This pattern of carelessness might be called neglect.

Both momentary carelessness and neglect can create giants.

FIVE UNDERLYING CAUSES
OF CARELESSNESS

What causes us to become careless or neglectful? There are at least five causes.

Cause #1: Impatience

Sometimes carelessness stems from impatience. We look for a faster, easier way to get a job done. We all know the old axiom, "Haste makes waste." I know from personal experience that it does.

I was a graduate student during the Christmas season of 1968. I must admit that I never did catch the Christmas spirit that season because all I could think about was studying for exams and writing a dissertation. My wife repeatedly encouraged me to back off the schoolwork and enjoy Christmas with our sons, who were then ten and eight years old. I didn't take her advice. Instead, it was all study, study, study for me.

We had a custom of taking down our Christmas tree the week after Christmas. I kept putting off that chore until finally Carolyn and the boys took down the tree by themselves. Then, Carolyn asked me to take down the outside Christmas lights that we had strung around the house. I agreed with her that it was a good idea to do so, but I kept delaying until finally it was New Year's Eve.

If the job was going to be done before New Year's Day, that was the time. The temperature had dropped to the low twenties so you can imagine how much I was dreading getting outside on a ladder. I suggested to Carolyn that we just leave the lights up and be one step ahead next Christmas. She didn't buy the idea. So I got a ladder, hammer, screwdriver, and pliers and decided to get it over with.

It was cold. I mean *real* cold. I took the screwdriver and put it under a staple holding the wire and pulled on the wire. A dozen or so staples popped out of the trim, and I thought, *Wow, that's the key. Just get hold of the wire and pull. There's no need to take each staple out one by one. Think of all the time I'll save.*

So I pulled hard on the wire, and before I knew it, forty feet of Christmas lights had fallen from the roof to the driveway. Every light on the string was shattered. I climbed down the ladder as quickly and as quietly as I could, hoping to scoop up the mess and put away the light cord before Carolyn could see what had happened. Unfortunately, my very thoughtful wife came outside at just that moment to bring me a cup of hot chocolate.

What timing! In trying to save a few minutes, not only had I made a mess, one that would require replacing lights the next season, but I felt stupid.

That was a minor incident to be sure, but it illustrates a point that is common in our world: in our hurry, we often create problems for ourselves. The person who darts in and out of traffic in trying to beat a light or save a few minutes of drive time may very well find himself in an accident. The person who invests in a project in hopes of making a quick buck and fails to thoroughly investigate the deal may very well find herself at the tail end of a scam. The person who takes shortcuts may very well find himself cut short.

Don't try to cram too much into your schedule.

Take your time. Be diligent. Don't try to cram too much into your schedule. You'll have fewer giants to face as a result of carelessness.

Cause #2: Greed

Sometimes a desire for monetary gain can drive us toward carelessness. Here in Myrtle Beach, South Carolina, where I live, the sport of bungee jumping became very popular a few years ago. Several bungee jumping locations were set up in our area, and for a cost of $65 to $75, a person could experience the thrill of jumping off a one-hundred-foot platform with nothing but a bungee cord tied around the ankles. I never saw what attracted people to this activity, but hundreds of people flocked to the bungee jumping locations every weekend.

In the summer of 1993, an elevator at one of the jumping areas wasn't working properly. Rather than shut down the site so a proper repair could be made, someone rigged a cable from another ride on the premises to lift the elevator, so that money could continue to be made.

Stay alert.

■

■

On a fateful day in the following week, the replacement cable broke loose as the elevator neared the top. The elevator cab crashed to the ground. Two teenage boys in it were killed—one of whom was with his family from Michigan, who watched the plunging elevator in horror. The crowd was stunned and devastated.

For the sake of a few dollars, carelessness resulted in a giant of a loss.

Cause #3: Distractions

Several years ago I was flying out of Detroit to Bismarck, North Dakota, on Northwest Airlines. It was a weekend, and as we waited in the airport, a special news bulletin flashed across the television screens in the airport. Northwest's flight 295 had crashed on takeoff in Detroit. Hundreds of people lost their lives. The investigation later revealed that the crew had neglected to put down the flaps. Nobody knows what may have distracted those crew members just long enough so that they overlooked one step in their takeoff sequence. But very often, a simple distraction causes us to be careless. A giant of a problem can result.

Ted Bundy, one of the most widely known serial killers of all time, stated that he looked for victims who were "inattentive." Muggers and rapists have told prison officials that they consider people who seem to be daydreaming to be easy targets. Car jackers have been interviewed on television programs saying that the easiest marks are those who don't seem to be paying attention to what is going on around them.

Stay focused. Stay alert. Don't allow yourself to become distracted or disoriented. Your not paying close attention can result in an attack from a giant!

Cause #4: Bad Advice

Recently, five teenagers were involved in an automobile accident while they were on their way to school. What happened? The student who was driving pulled out onto a highway at the encouragement of a motorist who gestured that the road was clear, even though neither the student nor the other driver could see clearly. A truck with a concrete mixer hit the car, killing four of the five students and causing severe brain damage in the fifth young person.

The young driver took bad advice. Rather than wait until he could determine the safety of the situation for himself, he relied on someone else for direction and guidance. Though there are times when we need to trust others for guidance, in nearly all cases, we are wise to take the time to check out that advice with a third party or to get a second opinion.

Carelessly taking bad advice can result in a giant of a problem.

Cause #5: Wrong Assumptions

Years ago, I was checking out a .22-caliber rifle. Thinking it was empty, I pulled the bolt back twice, and not aiming the rifle at anything in particular, I released the trigger. BANG! A bullet was in the chamber. It missed my son by just inches. I felt so nauseous at what had nearly happened that I haven't touched a gun since then. Just thinking about that incident makes me feel sick.

Wrong assumptions can result in giants.

AVOIDING THE GIANTS
OF CARELESSNESS

Some giants we create for ourselves by what we do. Others we create by what we *don't* do.

When we fail to do the five things on the following list, we can turn ourselves into giant bait. On the other hand, when we do these things, we put ourselves on a track where we are much less likely to face the totally unexpected, devastating problems that can kill us both physically and emotionally.

1. Take your time. Do every task in your life with diligence and care.
2. Pay the price. Don't let yourself be enticed by greed or "easy money" ploys.
3. Stay focused. Don't allow yourself to be distracted when you are engaged in a task that has any degree of danger associated with it.
4. Check out the advice you are given. A popular saying among carpenters is, "Measure twice and cut once." That's good advice for everything. Get two opinions before you take a major step.
5. Don't assume. Be sure.

Keep in mind that the results of carelessness go beyond the direct and real consequences that may be suffered to include inner emotional baggage. In the case of the Christmas lights, my inner emotional baggage included feeling stupid. The baggage might also include a load of guilt or a bundle of self-doubt.

When we are careless and the consequences of our carelessness result in problems, we nearly always think less of ourselves. Not only have we allowed a giant to emerge where none existed, but we have set ourselves up for a heavy dose of grasshopper mentality with which to fight the resulting giant. We beat up on ourselves as much as the giant beats up on us.

If you become the victim of your carelessness,

- apologize to any person you have hurt, including yourself. Don't try to justify what you have done. Admit your fault.
- make amends as best you can. Sometimes that might mean paying for damages. It may even mean community service. Penitence is not necessarily something to be avoided. It can be part of the healing process for other victims and of putting yourself into a position where you can truly forgive yourself.

- make a change in your habits. Recognize the element of carelessness that led to the problem and work hard at changing the way you go about doing things.

At least one thing is worse than suffering the consequences of carelessness, and that's suffering a second time for the same act of carelessness.

CARELESSNESS OVER TIME IS NEGLECT

Over time, carelessness can become a habit. Generally, that habit is one we can describe in part as being neglectful. Neglect has both short-term and long-term results. It is at the root of many people's problems.

We neglect to take care of our bodies. And we have a long-term health problem.

We neglect to take care of our month-to-month finances. And we have a major financial problem.

We neglect to tell our children or our spouses that we love and appreciate them. And we have a family problem of estrangement.

■

Take care in order to stay strong.

■

We neglect the basics of spiritual life. And we find that we have growing doubt and a growing lack of joy, peace, and hope.

When we are careless in any area of our minds, we build a pattern of neglect that results in damage to us.

Take care of yourself today. Take care of your relationships with people and with the Lord. Not only will you waylay some giants and keep them from appearing in your life, but you will be building yourself up so that you have a positive mind-set, health, and inner fortitude to face giants that are not of your own creation or neglect.

Take care in order to stay strong. Feed your spirit, mind, and body the right nourishment. Develop the habits that build character and result in success. You'll be in a much stronger position as a person—to enjoy times of peace and harmony in your life and to survive times of crisis.

CHAPTER 14

Keeping
the Mind
Pollution Free

Regardless of your political viewpoints or affili-
ation, you probably agree with most Americans that former president Ronald Reagan is
an optimist. His favorite stories reflect optimism. He loves to
tell about people who have achieved or who have overcome
impossible odds.

Where did Ronald Reagan acquire his optimistic outlook
on life? Most likely from his parents.

■
**Turn off the
television.**
■

As a child, President Reagan asked his
mother, "Are we poor?" His mother replied,
"You are only poor if you think you are." President Reagan's mother was a positive thinker
who looked on the bright side of life. She taught
her son that he should not feel sorry for himself,
and that he could have what he wanted if he was determined
to reach the goals he set. President Reagan credits his father
for teaching him that *what* a person wants is more important
than knowing *who* can help.

Throughout his radio, acting, and political careers, President Reagan held firm to these basic beliefs that a successful
life, a better attitude, a brighter outcome, and a more positive
opinion were not only possible, but achievable. Of equal

value, no doubt, was the fact that he refused to allow negative polls, circumstances, or critics to pollute his mind with
rubbish.

ATTITUDINAL POLLUTANTS

We have heard a great deal in recent years about environmental enemies. As a school administrator a few years ago,
I was very much concerned with asbestos in our school buildings.

As an educator, however—and as a parent and grandpar-
ent—I am much more concerned about the pollution of our
minds, our attitudes, and our value systems.

U.S. News and World Report ran an article entitled "What
Entertainers Are Doing to Your Kids." It told how America's
young people are having their minds polluted by external
stimuli on a daily basis. Some of the information in the article
was frightening:

- Studies show that teenagers listen to an estimated 10,500
  hours of rock music between the seventh and twelfth
  grades alone—just five hundred hours less than the total
  time they spend in school in twelve years.
- Songs aimed at the teen market have explicit lyrics about
  drugs, suicide, and various sexual acts including incest.
- Critics have counted an average of eighteen acts of violence in each hour of video.
- Television violence is so pervasive that the average student will have seen 18,000 murders in 22,000 hours of
  television viewing by the time he graduates. He will have
  watched television twice as many hours as he has spent
  in the classroom.

After I read this article, I began to think about the pollution of our children's minds. It isn't limited to what is
coming from television, videos, magazines, or newspapers,

as violent and obscene as some of those messages can be. Much of the pollution comes from homes and schools where children are constantly bombarded with messages that tell them they are worthless, incompetent, without a future, and of little value.

People continually claim that there is no scientific research to link television violence with real muggings and killings. We need to recognize that scientific studies rarely report cause-and-effect conclusions; rather, they report correlations. Two sets of behavior seem to exist together a high percentage of the time. The correlation between exposure to negative messages and negative behaviors is very high.

Furthermore, the Bible teaches that what people do is always directly the result of what they think and believe. Jesus taught,

> It is the thoughtlife that pollutes. For from within, out of men's hearts, come evil thoughts of lust, theft, murder, adultery, wanting what belongs to others, wickedness, deceit, lewdness, envy, slander, pride, and all other folly. All these vile things come from within; they are what pollute you and make you unfit for God (Mark 7:20–23 TLB).

It is precisely because we do what we think that the Bible teaches the importance of renewing our minds so that our behavior can be transformed. (See Rom. 12:2.)

Think back for a moment to the ten spies who saw themselves as grasshoppers in relationship to the giants of Canaan. Where did the spies get that opinion?

It wasn't from the facts alone. The more likely source of their grasshopper mentality was years and years—generations upon generations—of the children of Israel being slaves in Egypt. The Israelites had no concept of what it meant to rule, to reign, to conquer, to be strong, to defeat an enemy. They had a deeply entrenched mind-set of servitude, obeisance, groveling, bearing burdens, being stepped upon.

They had "pollutitudes"—polluted attitudes!

They needed a major overhaul in the way they saw themselves and others.

CLEANING UP THE TOXIC DUMP OF OUR MINDS

In many ways, the cleanup of our minds is similar to the cleanup of environmental toxic waste sites.

Stop the Flow of Toxins

We begin by turning off the inflow of poisons and trash. Turn off the television. Control what is heard and read and viewed in your home. Do this for your children and for yourself. Refuse to watch any behavior that you don't want to emulate. Refuse to listen to lyrics that depict behavior you wouldn't want to do or have done to you.

■ *Choose to be renewed in your mind.* ■

You may need to get away awhile—take a vacation to the mountains or the beach. Walk through nature and enjoy a different pace. You'll find it easier to turn off much of the negative media if you have put a little distance between it and yourself.

Ask for God's Help

Ask the Lord to cleanse your mind. Ask Him to drive away any remembrance of the negative images and words you have taken into your life. Ask Him to free you from any nightmares you may have experienced as a result of your polluting behavior. Ask Him to forgive you for putting your focus on things that are unlike Him and unworthy of His people.

Take In the Positive

Start putting into your mind positive thoughts, affirmations, music, and images. Choose to be renewed in your mind.

I like the advice that William Arthur Ward gives in this essay:

The IZE Have It

Here are seven simple ways to begin living a more abundant, exciting, productive, and rewarding life:

MEMORIZE at least one great truth every day. It may be an inspiring poem, an especially helpful verse of Scripture, an affirmation, or a favorite quotation. What you memorize becomes a part of your life, your character, and your future.

CRYSTALLIZE your goals, your aspirations, and your ambitions. Write them down and include a workable timetable for their accomplishment.

SPECIALIZE in some particular field of endeavor. Become an expert, and you will soon become indispensable. Become an authority, and you will inevitably become sought after.

NEUTRALIZE your fears, your doubts, and your anxieties through the power of prayer, meditation, and a positive mental attitude.

MINIMIZE your shortcomings, your liabilities, and your deficiencies. Because you were designed by a Master Architect, you are greater than you think.

MAXIMIZE your abilities, your talents, your potentialities, and your possibilities. Accentuate your positives.

RECOGNIZE the good in others, the beauty of friendship, the splendor of love, and the joy of service. Train your eyes to look for the best in others and invariably others will see the best in you.

In Philippians 4:8, we have this advice: "Whatever things are true, whatever things are noble, whatever things are just, whatever things are pure, whatever things are lovely, whatever things are of good report, if there is any virtue and if there is anything praiseworthy—meditate on these things."

We all know the saying, "You are what you eat." The fact is, we are also what we think about. Choose to think good things about yourself and about others.

YOU CAN CHOOSE YOUR ATTITUDE

Many people haven't come to this realization: you can choose your attitude. You aren't born with the attitude you have today. You acquired it. And if you acquired a bad attitude, you can change it and acquire a good one.

A fresh and positive attitude comes when we choose to see opportunities rather than defeats. It comes when we put our attention on the Land of Promise that stretches out before us rather than on the giants who presently occupy part of the land.

I enjoy telling the story of the two shoe salesmen who were sent to a newly discovered Pacific Island inhabited by primitive natives. Upon arriving, Salesman A called his home office and said, "Send the company plane down here right away and get me out of this place. There's no shoe business here. The natives are running around barefoot!"

Salesman B, on the other hand, called his home office with a radically different message: "Hey, boss, I found us a bonanza! Rush me all the shoes you can—all sizes, all styles, all colors. These poor natives are running around barefoot!"

Both salesmen faced the same circumstances. One chose to see a potential for good; the other saw only bad.

Amy was a young girl in the seventh grade, on the threshold of becoming a teenager. In a term paper, she wrote,

I always lose. You always win. I always fail. You always pass. I'm always last. You're always first. I'm always sitting around. You always have so much to do.

Well, I have been thinking about this a lot. And there just has to be something I can do. I think that when I find myself, I will also find a reason for living and a reason for dying and a reason for everything else.

Your ability to choose your attitude has a great deal to do with the way you define yourself. If you want to know who you are, evaluate what you think about yourself! In the seventh grade, Amy saw herself as a loser, a nobody, a failure. But she wasn't content with that definition of herself. She suspected there was something she could do—something she could win at, something she could succeed at, something she could enjoy. In that, there is hope for Amy. If you are in her shoes today, let me encourage you:

- Start seeing yourself as a potential waiting to burst open—not as an accident waiting to happen.
- Start seeing yourself as a treasure chest filled with talents and abilities—not as an empty safe that has just been robbed.
- Start seeing yourself as a free person with an unlimited future—not as a slave who longs to go back to slavery.

While I was traveling in New Zealand, I happened to notice a small sign in the window of a beachfront store. It read: "My name is Kelston Schalts and I want to work. I will give my best at anything offered me. I have no phone, but you can contact me at 70-B Beach Road or through the Oasis Store."

I ordered a hot fudge sundae, and when it was served to me, I asked the store owner how old the young man was who had written the note in his window. The owner replied that he was seventeen.

I said, "He must be quite a young man."

The storekeeper said, "He sure is. He had sought work from Auckland to Whangarei without any success. Two weeks after he put that ad in my window, he had a job. Your estimation of him was most accurate. He is an outstanding young man."

I have never met Kelston Schalts, but I suspect that he is going to go far in his life. He has chosen to have a positive "I'll give my best" attitude. He is reaching out to take hold of his life and define it in a positive way. He has a pollution-free attitude.

Choose today to overcome your grasshopper mentality. The decision to become a giant slayer begins in your heart and mind.

Thinking like a winner in the land of giants begins with a belief that you have inside you what it takes to kill a giant. Nobody can put that belief there but you. Nobody can force you to believe what you refuse to believe. Choose to believe today that you, with God's help, can take the land of promise and possibilities that He has designed for you.

CLEANSING THE MIND OF REAL CHEMICALS

Many of us also need to cleanse our minds in a literal way. I was shocked recently to read how many millions of Americans are taking antidepressant drugs. We seem to be a nation on tranquilizers. Those who aren't taking downers are often taking uppers to get themselves going. And then there are those who are taking drugs to even out their mood swings from down to up!

God didn't design our brains to run on manufactured chemicals. That isn't to say that we can't benefit from physician-prescribed medicines from time to time to help even out a chemical imbalance. But in the main, we seem to be a nation that is turning to chemicals too quickly and too soon as a means of resolving or eliminating every negative feeling we might have from time to time.

Rather than see ourselves as being sick—nervous, disoriented, hyperactive—perhaps we need to start thinking of ourselves as being well people who are in charge, with God's help, of our futures and our health.

I met a giant slayer in the lobby of a small airport in Kansas. The man had heart problems as his giant. At the age of sixty-two, Rollin had a heart attack and, shortly thereafter, major heart surgery. The aortic valve in his heart was replaced, and he had three bypasses. Sometime later, he needed to have that same valve replaced again and have two more bypasses. The mitral valve of his heart was reinforced, and he received a pacemaker. He later had a hemorrhage in the skull, partly owing to the blood thinners he was taking. He recovered. Just recently, he had his pacemaker replaced.

Be around people who point out the positive.

I met Rollin when he was seventy-eight years old—some sixteen years after his first heart incident. What made him a giant slayer? I believe a great part of his success was his attitude. I could tell within minutes after meeting this gentleman that he loved life. He was glad of the opportunity to get up that morning and drive five hours so that he could be in that airport. He was interested in the history of the airport and engaged in quite a lengthy conversation with the manager of the terminal about the airplanes that had been manufactured in Kansas during World War II. Rollin is embracing the joy of living. He sees himself not as a heart patient but, and particularly so on that day, as a former pilot, a farmer, a businessman, a father and grandfather, an alive human being.

Are you addicted to medication, drugs, or alcohol? If so, you probably started taking those things to help you face a giant in your life. Unfortunately, chemicals can become giants in our lives. Addiction to the things we take to help us harms us.

Are you relying on pills, drugs, or alcohol to help you face a giant? Change your behavior, and ask God to renew your mind so that you can face this giant without chemical assistance.

"MOVE" TO A CLEAN ENVIRONMENT

If you are suffering from mind pollution, you may need to move to a cleaner environment. That doesn't mean you need to relocate physically, although that may be advisable in some instances. That does mean you may need to find new friends and make new associations. You may need to change your relationship environment.

It's difficult to maintain a clean and healthful thought life if you are constantly around people who

- criticize others constantly, whether it's the government, the people next door, the behavior of family members, the boss, the children, the in-laws, the weather, the traffic. People who criticize nonstop spew toxic attitudes into your mind. Move away from them!
- tell lewd, rude, or racially and culturally biased jokes and stories. We once referred to such people as having their minds in the gutter. In today's terminology, we might say their minds are in the Dumpster or the toxic waste dump. Refuse to join them there.
- routinely use profanity. Exposure to a steady stream of profane words builds up inner anger that can explode in rage and abuse. Move away!
- are insulting or mean-spirited in what they say to you. Walk away from their insults. Don't let their words take root in you.

Be especially wary of those who do any of the above things with a loud voice. Those who yell or scream at us are especially toxic to our minds.

Choose, instead, to be around people who point out the positive, speak truth, are kind, and have a gentle spirit. You'll be healthier attitudinally.

The writers of the New Testament gave this advice numerous times:

So encourage each other to build each other up (1 Thess. 5:11 TLB).

Don't be too eager to tell others their faults, for we all make many mistakes (James 3:1 TLB).

Don't just think about your own affairs, but be interested in others, too, and in what they are doing (Phil. 2:4 TLB).

I need your help, for I want not only to share my faith with you but to be encouraged by yours: Each of us will be a blessing to the other (Rom. 1:12 TLB).

When we think of a person who suffered from polluting words, we probably think of Job. He faced genuine giants in his life. Satan targeted him for trouble. He lost all of his possessions and all of his children, and then he lost his health.

Three so-called friends came to Job with words of advice—toxic advice. One told Job that he must have done something wrong to be suffering so much, contending that the innocent don't suffer. Another questioned Job's relationship with God, since he believed that those in right relationship with God don't suffer. The third person claimed that Job must have had an evil heart, stating that those with evil hearts can never escape God's wrath.

Not one of those friends encouraged Job to believe God for deliverance. None of them stood by him without blaming him.

Job wisely rejected their counsel and cast himself entirely on God's mercy. The Lord not only reversed Job's situation—restoring to him health, family, and possessions—but He said to the friends of Job, "My wrath is aroused against you . . . for you have not spoken of Me what is right" (Job 42:7).

Stay in association with people who believe that they are winners in the land of giants, and that you can be one, too. Run from those who fill your mind with pollutants—negative ideas, words, and opinions that tear away at your confidence and the way you value yourself and others.

People with polluted minds rarely slay giants.

CHAPTER 15

Getting Out of the Sand Traps of Life

A giant doesn't necessarily mean a person, situation, or problem that looms to destroy you. A giant may be something that slows you down or impedes your progress.

One day after I had spoken at an event in Alabama, a principal came to me and said he had a golf story he wanted to tell me. He had been at a golf tournament and had decided to leave a little early because the day was so hot and humid. He walked by the practice area and noticed that one player was practicing wedge shots out of the sand trap. He watched the man's play for a few minutes as he went through the same motion again and again. He always got behind the ball and kept his eye on the pin. He addressed the ball the same way every time. The principal said that the golfer was making some incredible shots out of the sand trap so he decided to move closer for a better look.

To his surprise, he recognized the golfer—perhaps the most famous golfer of all time, Jack Nicklaus. To his greater surprise, upon finishing practice, Jack walked over to him and conversed with him for a few minutes about how important it is to prepare for the sand traps, both in golf and in life.

His point was well taken. Everyone, no matter how good a golfer or how good a person, ends up in the sand traps from time to time.

FOUR KINDS OF SAND TRAPS

What does a sand trap do to a golfer's score?

If a player knows how to use a sand wedge skillfully, the fact that the ball landed in a sand trap may not make a bit of difference to the score of a particular round. The hit out of the sand trap may just be the next stroke that takes the ball closer to the hole.

For the vast majority of players, however, landing in a sand trap sets back the score at least one stroke, especially if the sand trap is one lining a fairway. In hitting out of a sand trap, a player has a little less control and a whole lot less power on the ball.

For some players, landing in a sand trap can be a frustrating and score-devastating experience. I've seen players take three or more swings at a ball before they get it up out of the trap and onto the green or fairway.

From my experience, life's sand traps come in at least four varieties.

Sand Trap #1: Minor Setbacks

Some of life's sand traps come in the form of minor setbacks—the unexpected bill, the flat tire on the car, the tooth that needs filling, the bout with the flu.

We need coping skills to get out of these sand traps. Coping refers to the ability to handle, to deal with. In many cases, it means the ability to ride out the storm or to endure.

These setbacks are like giants who come to huff and puff at your door but have little power to blow your house down and destroy you unless you invite them to come inside and sit a spell.

I have a friend who once wrenched her back. The doctors could detect no problem with the spine. The best advice they could give was plenty of rest and patience. The pain persisted for about six months. Much of that time she spent lying in bed or walking, since being horizontal and being vertical were the only two positions remotely comfortable for her. Sitting for longer than fifteen to thirty minutes could be excruciating. I knew her to be very active so I asked her, "What did you do to cope with having to spend all that time in bed?"

She said, "I reminded myself of Psalm 23. Sometimes the Lord *maketh* us to lie down in green pastures. I decided that I would have to make the most of the time I spent lying in bed, so I read, listened to inspirational and educational tapes, and caught up on some overdue phone conversations with friends."

She had coping skills!

Successful coping includes the following:

> ■
> *Very often the best move we can make is to keep moving!*
> ■

- Maintain an attitude that things will work out. Envision the problem coming to an end. Anticipate the day when the problem will be resolved or the illness will come to an end. Believe for the day when the situation will turn around and things will start looking up.
- Refuse to give in to negative thoughts and emotions. Each time you have a negative thought, such as *I might never get better,* or *God must be punishing me for something,* or *I'm just a loser,* replace it immediately with a positive thought. Voice these thoughts aloud. Say, "I *am* going to get better," "I am going to learn something about this," "I am going to overcome this attack of the Enemy against my life," "I am a winner in Christ Jesus."
- Put the past behind you. You may have been responsible for the accident, been careless in a way that brought on the illness, or misjudged or miscalculated in a way that brought about the loss. Forgive yourself for making a mistake.
- Stay active. When we suffer a temporary setback, one of our first impulses is to sit down and have a pity party.

You may need a few minutes, hours, or days to get over a particular hurt, but the time comes when you need to get up, dust yourself off, and move forward.

As a coach, I saw players time and again suffer from charley horses. Their muscles would cramp up, and the pain would be excruciating. The best thing to do for such a cramp, however, is to walk it off, to keep moving or to have someone deeply massage the muscle right away. To sit down or lie down and hope the pain will leave does little good. The same holds for life's cramps. Very often the best move we can make is to keep moving!

Sand Trap #2: Lack of Organization

Sometimes we get bogged down in the game of life because we have let things get out of control. Our schedules, our environments, and our very lives lack organization so that we don't know which way to turn next. We are very vulnerable to attacks by giants at those times.

Organizing isn't limited to things. It includes organization of time and resources. Part of reorganizing our lives for success may very well involve delegating or entrusting others with various chores or tasks that we have taken on and that are bogging us down.

> ■
> **Get your prayer life in order.**
> ■

Moses was in this situation. In Exodus 18:13–27, we read that Moses' father-in-law came to visit him and found Moses judging the people from morning until evening. He asked Moses what he was doing, and Moses replied that the people were coming to him when they had difficulties so that Moses could judge each situation and make known to the people the statutes of God.

Moses' father-in-law, himself a great leader among his people, replied, "The thing that you do is not good. Both you and these people who are with you will surely wear yourselves out. For this thing is too much for you; you are not able to perform it by yourself." His advice was threefold:

1. Moses was to pray for the people before God.

2. Moses was to teach the people as a whole the statutes and laws of God, and to show them the way they should walk and the work they should do.

3. Moses was to select others who feared God, hated covetousness, and were truthful to be "rulers" over groups of people and to provide judgment when it was needed.

Moses' father-in-law helped Moses completely reorganize his life and the way he led the people. Moses heeded his advice, and as a result, Moses no doubt maintained the energy and strength he needed for the next several decades of leading the people through the wilderness.

Are you bogged down because you aren't properly organized? Are you frustrated from dawn to midnight because you have too much to do and too little time? Reevaluate your life, and see which parts you might let go and which tasks you might delegate or entrust to others. Get your prayer life in order, and make it your first priority. Decide what you are truly trying to accomplish, and focus on that. Then, train others to help you and to work with you so that you and they can be successful.

We all know that it's hard to run in sand. Being disorganized is like running in sand in your life. You expend a lot of energy but have little forward motion. It's tough to outrun a giant if you're in a sand trap of confusion and disarray.

Sand Trap #3: Bad Habits

Nearly all of us can identify one or more bad habits that slow us down, trip us up, or keep us from reaching our full potential. If bad habits aren't faced and dealt with, they can become addictions, obsessions, or illness.

Make a list of the habits you want to break. In doing so, you are facing up to them. Admit that not only do you have the habit, but it has you.

Make a second list of the habits you want to acquire. As much as possible, match up your first list with the second. For example, breaking the habit of being late for work might be coupled with the habit of getting to bed earlier and getting more sleep.

Attempt to break only one bad habit at a time. If you try to change your entire life, you will quickly become discouraged and give up. Make one change at a time.

Strive to understand the reason for your behavior. Were you taught incorrectly? Are you trying to run from a particular problem? Is your habit designed to cover a fault or assuage guilt? Get to the core reason for doing what you do.

If you need help in breaking the habit, seek it. You may need some professional advice in a particular area. You may need to ask your family or friends to help you. You may want to seek out a support group of others who are trying to break the same habit. You may need information about how to break a habit. Or you may need someone to encourage you as you attempt to change your behavior.

Substitute a good habit for a bad one. Use your two lists here. In breaking one habit, you must immediately substitute a new habit for it. For example, if you are going to lose weight, you are going to need to eat less and exercise more. Substitute the habit of exercise for the habit of overeating. Take some of the time you normally spend at the dinner table out walking in your neighborhood. Preferably, walk first and then eat. You'll be less hungry.

In breaking the habit of smoking, find something constructive to do with your hands and the time you normally spent puffing on a cigarette. One woman I know took up needlework. She even kept a small piece of embroidery in her desk at work, and during the times when she would normally spend five or ten minutes with a cup of coffee and a cigarette, she'd pull out her embroidery. Several months after her last cigarette, she had finished a beautiful embroidered scene that she framed and kept in her office. It was a reminder that she had done something constructive with time that would otherwise have gone up in expensive smoke.

Establish immediate and interim goals for yourself, with the ultimate goal being the complete break of the habit. You may have a habit of drinking too much caffeine in a day. As a start, you might shift to at least half decaffeinated coffee, tea, or cola in a day. Gradually decrease the amount of caffeine, and increase the percentage of decaffeinated beverages.

Set a reward for yourself. Give yourself a treat when you realize that you have won the battle against the bad habit and have reached your goal. Of course, you won't want to treat yourself to a cigarette if you have broken the habit of smoking, or celebrate your victory at a bar if you have overcome an alcohol problem. Choose a reward that is positive and that reinforces your new habit-free life.

> ■
> *Bad habits are sand traps.*
> ■

Stay out of situations that are likely to trigger a temptation to revert to the old habit. The Lord's Prayer has the line, "Do not lead us into temptation, but deliver us from the evil one" (Matt. 6:13). Once you have overcome a bad habit, recognize that part of your deliverance from evil is not putting yourself into a position of temptation. You could just as easily pray, "Deliver me from evil, and don't let me come anywhere close to those things, people, or places that tempt me."

Bad habits are sand traps. Get out of them as quickly as you can.

Sand Trap #4: Depression

Perhaps the most insidious sand trap of all is the deep discouragement and despair we know as depression. Depression comes in many varieties, from feeling a little down on a particular day to clinical depression that might result in hospitalization.

An estimated four to ten million Americans suffer from depression that is so severe they need psychiatric care. When depression is that severe, a person quickly loses touch with reality. Feelings of hopelessness and self-deprecation are devastating. Needless to say, it is very very difficult to respond positively to adversity or to face giants when a person is feeling depressed.

Often, depression is cyclical. The more depressed a person

becomes, the less able a person is to cope with problems, and therefore, the problems intensify or grow. The bigger the problem, the more overwhelming it appears and the deeper the depression becomes. The deeper the depression, the less ability to face life. And so on until the downward spiral results in a total inability to do the simplest things.

Falling into depression is like being in a sand trap and hitting the ball repeatedly, only to find that your ball catches the top of the sand trap and falls back into the trap once again. When that happens, a golfer usually has to walk around a bit, clear his mind, and then try something new with his swing. Hitting the ball the same old way just won't cut it.

The same is true for the sand trap of depression. You may need to reprogram your mind.

A friend of mine once said, "The spirit of man sometimes falls into moods of depression or doubt. But a person can usually fight his way out of that state by keeping his mind fixed on the top, by striving to make just one less mistake a day, and by swinging away the best he knows how."

Note the three things this friend suggests:

1. Keep your mind on the top. Think about the way things can be. If you are in a hole, don't look down or straight ahead. Look up!
2. Strive to take just one forward step a day. Don't try to do everything at once or have a perfect day. Try to make one less mistake tomorrow, and then one less mistake the next day. Give yourself a little time to get better.
3. Keep swinging. Don't give up and walk away from the game. Hang in there and keep trying.

A number of techniques can help you as you "keep swinging."

Find a way to express your inner feelings. For some people, writing down their feelings helps them to become more focused about the future and to feel as if they have been set free of the past. For others, talking to a trusted person can be a form of release that helps them develop a new way of thinking and feeling.

Envision a future you want to have that is realistic for you to attain. Visualization is a technique that is often used to help people who are depressed. Imagining oneself in a healthy, normal, beautiful environment can be a first step toward developing a healthy, normal, beautiful future. Make certain that the future you envision is something that is attainable and something that is in keeping with God's Word.

Accept the prayers of others and believe God to answer both their prayers and your own prayers for your future well-being.

Read your Bible and underline every promise of God that you read. Consider how those promises pertain to your life.

Listen to encouraging words. Tune out the negative, which may mean turning off the television set awhile. Listen to people who speak positive words of faith and encouragement. One way you might encourage yourself is to listen to praise music that lifts up the name of Jesus.

Don't let yourself think in terms of absolutes, such as "always" and "never." The depressed person often believes that things will *never* get better and that he or she will *always* be depressed. Not so! Change is possible. Emphasize that truth to yourself.

Do things that make you laugh. The theologian and philosopher Kant once said, "It is God's will, not merely that we should be happy, but that we should make ourselves happy." Depressed people nearly always have lost their ability to laugh at the foibles and follies of life. Do your best to regain your sense of humor!

And finally, *start speaking positively to yourself about yourself.* Don't build a case against yourself by putting yourself down, calling yourself names, denying your successes and good qualities, or comparing your weaknesses to other people's strengths. The depressed person nearly always speaks of himself in negative terms.

Start emphasizing your positive points to yourself! Give voice to your statements of self-appreciation and self-valuation so that your own two ears can hear them, take them in, and start believing them to be true. If you say about yourself what the Bible says about you, you won't be bragging or stretching the truth. Rather, you will be telling the truth to yourself.

Don't beat yourself up for getting discouraged or depressed. That will only make things worse. Everybody gets down occasionally. The point is, successful people refuse to *stay* down.

If you are living with a person you believe is suffering from depression, get help for that person. Watch for these symptoms:

- A sense of feeling unimportant
- Nearly constant anxiety
- Loss of interest in friends and family
- An inability to concentrate
- Feelings of guilt
- Indecisiveness
- Frequent crying and exaggeration of minor problems
- An alteration in normal eating and sleeping patterns

Don't delay. Confront what is happening, and get help as early in the cycle of depression as you can. The recovery time will be shorter and more successful.

■

Cultivate cheerleaders in your life.

■

Depression is sometimes triggered by hormonal or chemical imbalance. At other times, it is triggered by memories or dreams of difficulties in the past. The causes of depression vary, as do the means of treatment. Few of us are able to diagnose ourselves or those we love, and to help ourselves and others totally on our own.

Again, get help. In the case of depression, you need to change your swing to get out of the trap. And nearly always, you can benefit by having another golfer suggest how you might change that swing.

It's not a failure to get help. It's a failure to stay in the trap.

YOU CAN USE A GOOD PEP SQUAD WHEN YOU ARE IN A SAND TRAP!

As a coach who worked with high school teams for many years, I know the advantage of a team having a rousing pep band and very vocal cheerleaders. As far as I was concerned, the pep band members and cheerleaders were part of the team. They provided the boost that put us over the top in many a tightly fought contest.

When are the pep squad members needed the most? When the team is behind. When you have lost yardage. When you have suffered a major setback. That's the time when cheers mean the most.

I remember a conversation my wife and I had with Dr. Norman Vincent Peale. He and I were scheduled to speak as part of the same program, and Dr. Peale indicated how nervous he was. Carolyn said, "You can't tell me that after speaking for fifty years, you still get nervous."

He replied, "I have to fight it every day."

Everybody has sand traps to overcome—some of us on a daily basis. Even the best golfers find themselves in sand traps, and even the best speakers and performers find themselves with bouts of nerves.

In those times, you need to have somebody around who can cheer you on. Cultivate cheerleaders in your life. Associate with those who believe in you, value you, encourage you, lift you up when you are down, help you see a brighter tomorrow. And in turn, be their encouraging friend. Let encouragement flow like a two-way street between you.

Do you give encouragement to others with a teaspoon or a bucket?

THE MAGIC BUCKET AND DIPPER

According to an old story, each of us has an imaginary dipper and a bucket. They are invisible, but nonetheless real. When our buckets are full, we feel great. And most of us start out each day with full buckets.

The "magic" part of this bucket and dipper is this: when we make a positive comment or give a smile, pat of encouragement, or compliment to someone, we are dipping into our buckets and giving something of ourselves away. We help fill another person's bucket, but magically, we do not have any less in our buckets.

On the other hand, when we cut down, put down, or tear down someone else, we are dipping from that person's bucket. We can't, however, put what we dip into our own buckets. We must throw it away. No one gains and one loses.

The tendency is for the person who has been "dipped into" to respond with a dip of his own. Very quickly, both buckets can become dry.

Some have estimated that people tend to dip negatively into other people's buckets eight times more than they fill the buckets of others with encouraging words. How sad!

It costs you nothing to give a compliment or word of encouragement to someone else today. It can cost you dearly to give a word of discouragement or pain.

Choose to play life's game with people who can cheer you on when you hit the sand traps, and in turn, be a person willing to cheer others on when they hit a sand trap. Together, you can make it through the course!

CHAPTER 16

Filling the Cup—
And Keeping
It Full!

S ometimes a giant isn't an enemy. It may loom large, and it may appear ominous, but the giant is actually a bigger opportunity, a blessing still in disguise.

Imagine for a moment that you are like a cup of water. Then suddenly you are emptied into a quart container. As a cup of water, you may feel rather insignificant as you slosh around in the bigger container. You may feel small, weak, a "nothing." Your challenge, however, is not to get out of the quart container and back into a cup measure but to fill up the quart container. Yours is an opportunity to grow, to expand, to develop, to multiply, to learn, and to become more of who you were created to be!

Every person who is on the rise—no matter the profession, field, or endeavor—is going to face experiences that stretch him or her. Every success story in the making is going to be marked by upward steps that represent bigger challenges and which often involve greater risks and problems. The challenge is not to rail against the opportunity but to rise to the occasion—to fill up the larger cup and keep it full, ever expecting to be poured into yet a larger container.

One man who has done this throughout his life is Lester

M. Alberthal, Jr., president, chief executive officer, and chairman of the board of directors of EDS (Electronic Data Systems Corporation).

Founded in 1962, EDS today has revenues of almost $10 billion and profits in excess of $800 million. More than 80,000 employees serve customers in more than thirty-five nations. The company is an acknowledged leader in the information business, specializing in how information is created, distributed, shared, enjoyed, and applied. EDS is unabashedly gunning for the unofficial title of "World Technology Leader."

Les Alberthal became president and chief executive officer of EDS in 1986 and was elected chairman of the board of directors in 1989. He is widely recognized as one of the top executives in the world.

On the personal side, I don't know a nicer man than Les. He's easy to talk to and pleasant to be around. In 1994, he was named Dallas's "Father of the Year." He has received the Henry Cohn Humanitarian Award of the Anti-Defamation League. He serves on a number of boards and advisory committees, and yet, for all he is and does, he's one of the most down-to-earth men I've ever met.

I was privileged to visit with Les in his offices at EDS several years ago, and then again fairly recently. EDS's physical plant is one of the most impressive I have ever seen. Having had the experience of being a school superintendent of a district with several hundred teachers, who in turn impacted thousands of students, I was impressed with the sheer magnitude of Les's job. Each morning when he goes to work, the decisions he makes impact more than eighty thousand families, which represent more than a quarter of a million people. His influence is tremendous. He faces a daily challenge of not only making wise fiscal decisions but of motivating his employees and of creating a healthy and secure environment for them in which to work—one that is beneficial financially, psychologically, and emotionally.

He's a man who has faced and conquered repeated challenges to "keep the container full."

Running a corporation like EDS would be a giant to virtually anybody, regardless of their background. But if you look at the place where Les Alberthal started in life—the tiny town of Comfort, Texas—you may very well conclude that a person just can't get there from here. Nothing in Alberthal's childhood seemed to indicate that the chairmanship of one of the largest and most influential companies in the world was to be part of his destiny.

How is it he fills and fulfills his many current roles? What were the building blocks of his life? What is it that went into filling his cup in the first place?

NO SUBSTITUTE FOR BASIC INGREDIENTS

Les grew up in an environment where personal pride, the work ethic, basic family values, and Christian beliefs were important. His family was far from rich in terms of money. In fact, from Les's perspective, in that small town not having money wasn't an issue, because nobody had any money. He was rich, however, in ethics and values, which were established at home and then reinforced by the community—the churches, the town leaders, and the school system. In many ways, he feels as if he was raised by his entire town because the people of Comfort all seemed to have the same core beliefs.

As a young person, he had limited exposure to the outside world. Nobody in his family had ever gone to college, and as a teenager, Les didn't have a great deal of confidence that he was college material. The idea of going to college simply wasn't discussed much and certainly wasn't pushed. Most of the young people in the area went to work on family farms and ranches, and very few built careers based on a college degree.

Les's first step after high school was to go to San Antonio, the closest big city to his hometown, where he went to business school for a year and a half. For him this was a bigger container—one he eventually filled. While in San Antonio, he met Cliff and Ethel Hedman, who provided him the encouragement to try college. "They basically told me that there was not a reason that I *couldn't* get a college education if I wanted one," he said, "and that a college degree would open up doors of opportunity. That small amount of encouragement caused me to come to the conclusion that if I was going to have any opportunity to succeed professionally or financially, I was going to have to earn a college degree."

Les overcame any feelings of inferiority he may have had and poured himself into a bigger container called the University of Texas. He worked his way through school. His parents helped him as much as they could, but Les held three to five part-time jobs at any one time and took a full course load. It wasn't easy, and he doubted himself on more than one occasion. But he stuck with his plan and succeeded.

The building blocks of good family and church values, a solid work ethic, and the encouragement of others were also linked to the encouragement that Les gained from books. During his high school and college years, he read all of the books that Dr. Norman Vincent Peale wrote, and he tried to put Dr. Peale's encouraging concepts into practical use. "I had to take it literally a day at a time and a piece at a time," Les said, "but as each day went past, I could see progress was being made, however small it was." Eventually, he conquered the giant called college.

After graduating from the University of Texas in 1968 with a degree in business and accounting, Les landed a job with EDS. He was drawn to the company because it seemed to value individual contribution, and all its stated purposes were ones that meant a great deal to him.

Coming from a rural background and not having traveled much, Les once again found himself in a larger container. He felt inferior to his peers. He knew that he needed to add experience to his college degree, as well as exposure to the world. He didn't care a great deal in those early years where he lived, whether he had to travel, whether he got vacation at prime times, or even if he took vacation. He went and did what was asked of him, feeling it was excellent training and personal development. The result was that in a short period of time, he gained a great deal of experience and exposure.

"When I joined the company it took about six months before I figured out that the only people that were really listened to were the officers of the company," Les recalls. "So at age twenty-three, I set a goal to be an officer of the company by the time I was thirty. I missed that goal by a couple of months. But other than that goal, I have never set a goal regarding position. My goal was only to maximize my level of contribution to the company. Fortunately, I was rewarded well for the contributions I made."

■ **Part of sizing up the situation involves being honest with oneself.** ■

Les worked his way to the top. Within three years after joining EDS, he was made an account manager. Three years later he became a vice president with responsibility for the health care division. He was named a senior vice president in 1979 with responsibility for the insurance group, the largest operating group in the company. When EDS was acquired by the General Motors Corporation in 1984, he led all of the non-GM North American operating groups. Les moved to bigger and bigger containers, and each time he filled them to the brim.

WHAT GOES INTO FILLING THE BIGGER CONTAINER?

What are the basics to being successful, to filling the bigger opportunities in which one finds oneself? Les believes strongly in three: 1) a tremendous amount of hard work, 2) a lot of long hours, and 3) persistence—recognizing that success isn't going to happen overnight.

He adds to that the basics of character. "I had a coach in high school who really drilled into me that if you execute the basics correctly and proficiently, then you will be competitive," he says. "And to the degree that a person executes those basics better than another person in business, they are going to be more competitive and more successful. I am not enamored with great theories and philosophies of business. In a business like EDS, which provides professional services, the basics are the way in which we deal with our customers and our people. If we deal with people in a straightforward, candid, honest manner, that is going to be the difference between success and failure."

Part of sizing up the situation also involves being honest with oneself.

■

No one set of rules fits all opportunities.

■

"A person has to deal with himself or herself in the same way," Les contends. "Individually, you have to be honest and candid with yourself—determine what it is you want to accomplish, what you want to do and be, and then be a very strict but fair critic of yourself. You have to come to grips with balancing what you want to be and what price you are willing to pay to get there. If you are not willing to spend the effort and time for a certain level of success that you want, then what you want to *be* versus what you are willing to *pay* is out of balance. The person who is out of balance is going to be very unhappy and is likely going to try to find someone else to blame for his unhappiness. That's where being a severe but fair critic comes into play. The people I know who have been most successful have had an ability to be honest with themselves."

Les makes no claim to having a magic formula for balancing career and family. As virtually every person knows, a family could easily take twenty-four hours a day, seven days a week. The same for a career. Again, it's a balancing act. But one thing Les has learned to do is to turn his harsh criticism of himself into a series of positive, corrective action steps. When he doesn't like something he sees in his life, he finds a way to say, "Self, it's now time to get positive and do something about this." If he finds his life out of balance, he says, "Self, it's time to make changes."

In his career, Les has faced numerous distinct challenges as his career expanded in size and scope. At one point, he faced the challenge of supervising people with whom he didn't have regular face-to-face contact. Another difficult moment came when he was named president of the company. Suddenly he was thrust into a position of being the leader of hundreds of people who just the day before had been his peers. Trying to be an effective leader without showing favoritism, intentionally or unintentionally, was tough. The point to be made is this: bigger opportunities always have unique and difficult angles and facets to them. No one set of rules or guidelines fits all opportunities. The basic approach one takes to these new opportunities, however, generally calls upon a person to dig deep into himself or herself, to draw upon the basics of hard work, persistence, long hours, honest self-appraisal, a readjustment of priorities, and an ability to make and follow through on positive, corrective action steps.

In Les's case, he says he frequently falls back upon his inner self and the foundation of basic values he received as a child. He says, "When faced with adversity or challenge of one sort or another, I look inward. I have always been able to fall back on those basic Christian and family values and go from that, sort things out, and come forward knowing what is right, what is wrong, and which way to respond. There's a strength in each one of us that comes from a higher source." It's his personal faith and inner fortitude that Les relies upon most to help him as he seeks to face and grow into a new opportunity. As a young person and college student, when he needed quiet time, he'd go to a church during the day and sit there by himself, or go into the woods where he could reflect in solitude.

In all, Les Alberthal doesn't look to just one thing that gave him a full cup of fortitude for facing life's new arenas. Rather, it's a lot of days, and a lot of years taken one step at a time, recognizing that experience and accomplishment take time and don't happen overnight. Patience and dedication don't happen in an instant. They take a lifetime to develop fully.

He also draws upon his friends and associates. Sometimes, he has noted, it only takes one inspirational word or phrase—or in some cases, a "kick in the pants"—to get things moving forward in his life. He draws upon colleagues at work, friends outside of work, his parents, his wife, and his three children.

There are a number of lessons to be learned from Les Alberthal's life. For me, the top eight are these:

1. He has never separated himself from the basic family, Christian, and personal values of his childhood. Lots of people try to run away from their pasts. He hasn't.

"But," you may say, "I didn't have a childhood like that." Well, it's never too late to adopt the values that can give you a foundation for your future. Basic beliefs in self-reliance, hard work, honesty, fair dealings, the importance of family, and a willingness to pay the price are values you can choose to adopt in your life today.

2. He made positive principles a habit. I feel quite confident that Les Alberthal doesn't even know what he does, on most days, to keep himself motivated. He has developed a large storehouse of positive ideas on which to draw.

3. He builds his tomorrows on the successes of today and yesterday. Les Alberthal doesn't expect something for nothing. His life has been built from one step to the next, from one level to the next.

4. He has learned how to motivate himself by being his own critic and then developing positive action steps for the negatives he sees in his life. What a wonderful ability this is for a person to develop. Self-criticism is not necessarily a negative thing. You can criticize yourself and assess yourself honestly. But then, move beyond that criticism to take positive steps that will raise you up from where you are, truly to where you want to be.

5. He has been willing to pay the price for success. It costs something to slay giants. It also costs something to tackle a new opportunity or receive a "bigger blessing." It requires

risk, effort, and sacrifice. Are you willing today to pay the price to live or work on a higher plain?

6. He surrounds himself with those things that renew him.

Everyone finds himself in a container that is drying up from time to time. But there's no excuse for allowing oneself to go dry. Get back to the basics. Surround yourself with people who love you and will give encouragement to you. Read or listen to those things that uplift you. Spend some time alone with your Creator.

Once after Dr. Norman Vincent Peale had spoken to my school system, he said to me, "Thanks for letting me be here with you, Billy. When I came here, my cup was empty, and you filled my cup."

Here was a man who had preached for fifty years, had written more than forty books, and was the very embodiment of positive thinking to millions of people admitting that on some days, his cup gets dry!

It's true for all of us, though. No matter how successful a person may be, there are some days when he or she feels down and discouraged. There are some days when he feels that nothing he does matters or that his life is without meaning. There are some days when she feels that her best days are in the past. When those days come, we need to put ourselves into a position to be filled up! If we allow ourselves to stay in a dry state, we are much more susceptible to developing a grasshopper mentality, and in turn, to making mistakes that can cause great damage—to ourselves, and in some cases, to others.

On another occasion when Dr. Peale and I were addressing educators in West Virginia, I had the opportunity to share with him my first meeting with Les Alberthal. I told him how Les carried a portion of his writings in his billfold and how much his books had influenced Les. Dr. Peale was genuinely encouraged.

■ **None of the great heroes of the Bible quit.** ■

On a recent visit with Les, I found him filling my cup. In reflecting on this on the flight home, I couldn't help but see a circular pattern. It's more than a matter of what goes around automatically comes around. In reality, it's a matter of what we give out to others, we are more likely to attract to our own lives. To keep our own cups full, we need continually to be finding ways of encouraging others to keep their cups full. And that is another attribute that speaks to me so strongly in Les's life:

7. He genuinely seeks to help others. Les isn't interested in fighting giants alone. Even being president, CEO, and chairman of the board, he can't do it all at EDS. Les is a team builder who desires the best for all the employees of EDS so that they might *together* enjoy a shared success. He is very concerned that individuals—without regard to race, religion, cultural background, or any other artificial marker— have the same opportunity he enjoys within EDS to maximize their contribution to the company and to reap both financial and psychological benefits accordingly. As former Comfort school superintendent Eddie Derr has said, "The key to Les is, he helps other people succeed."

To keep your cup full and then to fill up new and bigger containers, surround yourself with others from whom you can draw and to whom you can give.

It isn't enough to be a giant slayer on your own.

Think back to David for a moment. He slew Goliath, but he certainly couldn't have taken on the entire Philistine army on his own. He was the point man for the battle, but he needed the Israelite army backing him up if he was truly to be part of winning the war.

Finally, this goes without saying:

8. He doesn't give up. Les Alberthal, to my knowledge, has never given in to a challenge.

The old axiom is true: no matter how badly or how many times a person fails, he is never a failure providing he gets up just one more time than he falls down.

In one of his sermons, Pastor Michael Jackson of Bethel Assembly Church in Rapid City, South Dakota, says we should consider some of the key figures in the Bible:

Moses easily could have given up. He had a bad crime on his record, a physical handicap, a temper . . . *but he didn't give up.*

Joshua could have said, "We failed to enter into the Promised Land once. We've wandered around this wilderness now for forty years—I quit!" *But he didn't.*

Daniel, after having been a slave and having been tossed into a lion's den, could have said, "Everyone's against me. The king is trying to kill me. They don't want me to pray. Why, even the lions won't have anything to do with me. I'm done!" *But he didn't.*

David could have cried, "I am never going to get it together. Why try!" *But he didn't.*

Peter might have said, "After what I've said and done, what's the use! I quit. Count me out!" *But he didn't.*

None of the great heroes of the Bible quit. They always accepted and fulfilled the new challenge put before them.

PUTTING IT ALL TOGETHER

Throughout this book, we've focused on individual aspects of winning in the land of giants, but when you begin to put those principles to work in your life you are likely to find that they mesh as a whole. One principle about overcoming grasshopper mentality builds upon another. Each aspect of winning in the land of giants is linked to all other aspects.

No one ingredient fills the cup each and every time. It takes many ingredients, many points of inspiration, and many positive steps to fill a bigger cup and then to keep it full.

The good news is that none of these ingredients is beyond your ability to acquire them. Neither are they beyond your capability to use them!

CHAPTER 17

Taking a Hit

J J. Thomas was an outstanding professional boxer
in his day. I had the privilege of having Mr. Thomas
as my boxing coach when I was just a teenager.
He taught me the importance of being able to take a hit.

Two principles are involved in taking a hit when you are in
the boxing ring. The first is to go with the punch. If you lock
your jaw or neck into place to resist a punch, you risk being
badly hurt or even knocked out. You are likely to hear bells
ringing or have blurred vision, and your recovery time is going
to be far longer than if you move with the punch, which basically is moving away from your opponent in the same direction the punch is going. Another way of saying this is to roll
with the punch.

■
**Go with
the punch.**
■

The second principle in taking a hit is that a
good boxer never lets his opponent know how
much the hit may have hurt. I can still hear Mr.
Thomas telling his boxers after a hit to "shake
it off" and "get the cobwebs out of your head."
He taught us never to register the shocking pain
we were feeling. "If you do," the coach said, "your opponent
is going to move in for the kill and hit you even harder."

Every boxer needs to know how to take a hit because all
boxers get hit! There is no way to avoid getting hit.

The same is true in life. There is no way to avoid life's hits. In taking a hit, the important thing is not whether you fall down, but whether you get up and come back strong.

GETTING UP AND GOING FORWARD

One evening, several of us were watching a match when one of Mr. Thomas's boxers was knocked down. Mr. Thomas and all of the boxer's teammates began encouraging him to get up. Mr. Thomas always figured that a boxer should be able to regroup and recover his senses and strength by the count of eight. It was at the eight count that a boxer needed to make his move to get up and go on with the fight. It was obvious that the young fellow had the strength to get up and that he was still conscious. He didn't make a move, however, and took the full ten count, which meant that the referee awarded a knockout to the other fighter.

With a puzzled look on his face, Mr. Thomas asked, "Son, why didn't you get up at the count of eight like we were encouraging you to do?" The young boxer looked at him and said, "He would have just knocked me down again."

The young man never fought another fight. I've thought about him repeatedly through the years, and I've wondered on numerous occasions how he has handled the blows of life.

When we get hit, we may need to take a short breather. Animals do that when they are injured. They frequently slink away to a safe place to recover from their injuries. But then, they emerge again. That's the approach we need to take. When you are hit, give yourself some recovery time, but then get up again. Don't expect to get knocked down. Expect to strike a winning blow once you are back on your feet.

FOUR OF THE STRONGEST BLOWS

Four of the strongest blows any giant can ever deal you are these: (1) insults, (2) rejection, (3) false accusations, and (4) deliberate actions intended to destroy you. Each of these is a blow below the belt, which in boxing terms is an illegal blow, but one that some fighters throw and that can cause great injury, even death.

Blow #1: Insults

I know what it means to be insulted. As a child, I had teachers who thought that because I lived in a federal housing project, my future was limited. Numerous people told me that they didn't think I had what it takes, even to the point of labeling me a failure.

One professor said to me in an advanced math class at college, "There's nothing in your background that prepares you for this." I don't think he was trying to put me down. Rather, he was trying to convey to me that I didn't have the academic background to do the work. I had been struggling to try to keep up with those in the class who had already passed several years of mathematics courses. I was determined to compete at their level, but I was not succeeding at it. In a rather obtuse way, the professor was trying to comfort me by pointing out that I didn't have the same background in math that the others had. Nevertheless, his comments stung. They reminded me of all the failures associated with my past.

I don't fault the professor for being honest with me or for stating what no doubt seemed like the obvious to him. I don't fault him for trying to encourage me. What he failed to recognize, however, was the real value of my effort. He failed to note that I was determined to overcome my past deficiencies through drive and determination.

Several years ago, a study at the University of Chicago concluded that the five most significant factors that lead to high achievement in all walks of life are these:

1. Drive
2. Determination
3. Hard work
4. Encouragement from home
5. Encouragement from school

I grew up in a world that thought IQ (intelligence), social upbringing, and privileged status led to success. That was the message conveyed to me again and again by teachers and other adults in authority positions. According to the University of Chicago study, however, intelligence and socio-economic status aren't even among the top five factors!

We know today that parental care is far more important than socioeconomics. We know that hard work, drive, and determination allow a person to overcome deficiencies.

The professor didn't expect me to compete with the others, and he didn't think I should expect to compete with them. He failed to see that I had the drive and desire to compete and to succeed. And I did. I already knew I wasn't the smartest student—based on sheer intellectual firepower. But while other students were hanging out at the bookstore or the coffee lounge, ol' Billy was working, working, working. I had the drive to do well.

■

Expect to strike a winning blow once you are back on your feet.

■

The point is this: those who insult you don't know the inside you. Insults are always based on surface information. They aren't based on the truth of God's Word. They have nothing to do with the redemptive power of Jesus Christ's shed blood on the cross. They aren't remotely connected to the desires of your heart and the destiny of your soul.

Insults ultimately are no match for the power of a person's will if the person being insulted will only exercise his will with power. Never give in to an insult. Never carry it in your heart. If you do, it can eat you up inside and destroy the drive and desire that can carry you to your true destiny.

If giants come at you with insults, take the punch, but don't stay down. Get up and walk on with your head held high and even greater determination burning in your heart to succeed in fulfilling God's plan for your life.

Blow #2: Rejection

Millions of people in our nation are reeling from the blows of rejection. Those who are in the process of divorce or who have been divorced nearly always feel a sense of rejection. Those who have lost their jobs, regardless of the reason, feel rejected. Children feel rejected by parents they see as uncaring or abusive, and older parents often feel rejected by their children. All of us get hit with rejection at one time or other.

■

Those who insult you don't know the inside you.

■

Something we regard as a good idea, another person sees as a bad idea.

Something we want to share with another person, the other person doesn't want any part of.

Something we try to express, another person doesn't want to hear.

Rejection comes our way in all sorts of packages and forms. In taking the hit of rejection we need to keep one truth at the forefront of our thinking: people may reject us, but God won't.

We also need to make certain that we don't confuse rejection with judgment. Many of us feel judged when we are rejected or feel rejected when we are judged. The two are different.

Rejection is nearly always based on who a person is or isn't—or who the person is perceived to be or not be. A husband may reject a wife, or a wife a husband—not necessarily on the basis of what that person does but for who that person is. Rejection is nearly always rooted in likes and dislikes—opinions about a person that are based on past, appearance, race, age, and so forth.

Judgment, on the other hand, is based not solely on who you are but on what you do and on the choices you make. If you reject a person partly for his behavior, you are not simply rejecting him; you are also judging him.

God never rejects a person for who that person is. God created each of us and loves us as His creations. We are always welcome to enter His presence. He always longs to communicate with us and have a relationship with us. God does not reject His children.

That does not exclude God from judging, however. Our behavior is subject to His judgment.

God gives us a choice regarding eternal life. He gives us every opportunity to make the choice in a way that is to our favor and eternal benefit. He warns us openly of the consequences of a failure to make the wise choice.

As a coach, I graded players for their performance on the field. We would watch game films and sit down with the kids and grade their performance. In the process, they learned to grade themselves. Did the young man make the block? Did he kick the ball the right way? Did he execute the play well?

If every player did everything he was supposed to do in the right way, every play would have the potential to be a touchdown. But that isn't what happens. One or more players break down and don't do what the play called for them to do. Generally speaking, only a few plays in an entire game make the difference between losing and winning. And in nearly all cases, those particular plays involve one or more players slipping up. There might be a fumble, an intercepted pass, or a failure to block.

Now, in judging a player's performance, we never rejected a player as a person. We always thought the best of each young man and believed in his potential. But we did judge his efforts and his performance on the field.

The Bible teaches us that the day will come when we will face judgment for what we have done. When the Lord puts up the screen and plays back for us the game of our lives, we're going to see where we have failed. The Lord won't need to show us where we have made poor choices. They will be obvious to us. We'll know that we have sinned. Judgment will be readily obvious.

In the present tense of our lives, we shouldn't carry around wounded hearts when no wound was intended. A low grade from a teacher doesn't necessarily mean that the teacher doesn't like you, value you, respect you, or admire you as a person. It means that you earned a low grade on that particular exam.

A poor evaluation from a supervisor at work doesn't necessarily mean that your job is in jeopardy. It means that you need to make some changes in some areas and work harder, smarter, and perhaps with a new attitude.

A turndown in a relationship doesn't necessarily mean that the person hates you. It may mean that the person doesn't choose to engage in that particular project, be a partner in that venture, or go out on that date with you.

Don't automatically internalize another person's actions to mean rejection. Instead, recognize that not everybody is going to like everybody else. A person who loves you dearly won't desire to be with you every moment of every day.

Roll with the punch. But don't walk out of the ring. Stay in the relationship if at all possible. This is especially important if the other person is a fellow Christian. Strive for peace in your relationship. Keep the lines of communication open.

Blow #3: False Accusations

From time to time, others will accuse you falsely. Jesus taught that when this type of persecution comes for His name's sake, you are to rejoice. When you are falsely accused for your faith or accused for what you believe to be true, take the hit and roll with the punch. God has a reward in mind for you.

That does not mean you shouldn't work to clear your name. That does mean you shouldn't get so bogged down in attempting to clear your name that you get off track in doing what the Lord has called you to do. You are going to be falsely accused by people no matter what you do in some instances. It's better to stay true to your course than to get sidetracked in long processes of self-defense.

But make certain that you don't *invite* accusations.

The silversmiths in Ephesus tried to say that Paul and others in the church there were trying to destroy their business. A man named Demetrius led the accusations, saying that Paul had said, "They are not gods which are made with hands" (Acts 19:26).

When the issue came to a head in the theater at Ephesus, the clerk of the city finally quieted the crowd and made three major statements about the men who had been cited as representatives of the church:

1. He noted that the men had not robbed the temple of Diana. We can keep ourselves from accusation by not attempting to destroy those with whom we disagree. We need not ridicule them, rob their reputation, attempt to destroy them, or try to do them in. Paul didn't attempt to destroy the temple of Diana. Rather, he attempted to build up the living "temple" of God's people, the church at Ephesus. (See Eph. 2:19–22.)
2. He noted that the men had not blasphemed the goddess Diana. We keep ourselves from accusation by not speaking out against the objects of worship that our enemies may hold dear. Paul didn't rail against Diana. Instead, he preached Christ. We Christians don't need to denounce what is wrong, evil, or false nearly as much as we need to proclaim what is right, good, and true.
3. He said that the accusers should bring their cases to the courts if they had cases. We keep ourselves from accusation by fighting our battles through recognized legal channels.

In the end, we need to trust the Lord that right will prevail, and that He will be our Deliverer and Defender. Jesus is our Advocate in heaven. He stands on our side when we keep His commandments and put our trust in Him.

If false accusations come your way, roll with the punches as best you can. And keep proclaiming what you know to be right, and do what you know is right to do.

Blow #4: Deliberate Actions Intended to Destroy You

If people are intent on destroying you, they can nearly always find a way. When people come at you to take from you, rolling with the punch can mean giving them what they want and walking away.

It isn't necessarily the thing to do in all cases. But it certainly is the thing to do in many cases.

Police officers routinely advise potential mugging victims or women who fear rape, "Don't resist. You may lose your possessions or be violated, but you have a better chance of keeping your life if you offer no resistance." Though opinions vary on this advice, some people are alive today because they played dead or refused to resist when they were violently and willfully attacked.

A friend of mine is in the restaurant business, and every Wednesday he invites businessmen and women to one of his restaurants to have lunch and to hear an inspirational speaker. He invited me to speak one time. Prior to my speaking, he and I were in his office, and I asked my friend to pray about a business problem I was having. I had been wronged financially and was feeling deeply wronged personally in this situation. My friend is a man of powerful prayer, and he quickly agreed to pray about the situation.

He also told me a story from his personal life. He said, "Billy, let me tell you something. I entered a business relationship with a real nice man—one of the nicest men I had ever met—and before I knew it, he had signed my name to a bank note. The day came when the note was due, the man was gone, and everybody was looking to me to pay up. I decided to fight that thing. The amount due was just about the same as the loss your wife is facing. The longer I fought, the more I realized that I was losing, in more ways than one. Pretty soon, the attorney fees were up to $125,000. That was more than what others were saying I owed. I borrowed enough to pay off the attorneys and walked away from the fight. You can keep on rehearsing what has happened and nursing those ill feelings, and before you know it, you will be totally defeated. The defeat will not only be financial."

I argued, "But you have several restaurants. I can't afford to take a hit like this."

He said, "If you continue to fight it, the day will come when you can't afford *not* to settle it and walk away from it. There are those in business who know all the ropes. They know the underside of the belly of greed, and they are the people who come after honest men and women. They find people who have worked all of their lives to earn something, and they want what they haven't earned. When they get their hooks into you"—and at that point, he put his fingers under my collarbones as if to make his point about hooks—"they are prepared to reel you in. They will use you until you are fully spent. My advice to you is to pay your way out of this, walk away from it, and put it behind you."

Sometimes taking a hit means a knockout for that particular fight on that particular day. If that's the case, look forward with anticipation to the moment when you can step back in the ring and go for a rematch!

THE INABILITY TO TAKE A HIT

What happens if a person doesn't develop the ability to roll with a punch?

The results can be devastating.

Not too long ago, a neighbor took a gun and shot himself in the head because he couldn't see how he could survive a particular financial hit. The man was only forty-eight years old. He had a loving wife and family, and he had enjoyed success. He had his mind, his health, and financial skills that he could have used to recoup his losses over time. Instead, he fell into despair and took himself out of the fight.

In contrast, I have another neighbor who is rolling with a punch. He has taken a severe blow, but he is getting back up on his feet.

I met him one day while I was standing outside our house talking to a friend. He drove up in a white truck, and after our mutual friend introduced us and then left, the man said to me, "Do you have a couple of minutes for us to chat?" I said, "Sure."

He told me that he had been in counseling for a few months. Finally, he said, "Do you see this truck?"

I said, "Yep."

He said, "Look at the mileage." I looked and saw that the truck had more than 140,000 miles on it. He got big tears in his eyes and said, "This truck is all I own to my name."

I said, "Well, I hate to hear that."

He said, "Three years ago, I had $5.5 million in liquid assets. I took on a partner. I wasn't satisfied with what I had. Do you know that big house at the entrance to this development?"

I said, "Yes."

He said, "I built that house. That was my house. Do you know that lot over there where you are planning to build your new home? That was my lot. I had everything anybody could ever want, and I lost it all. The only way we're living here now is that my wife's father owns the townhouse we're in."

He went on, "Not only did I lose all our material wealth, but I lost my dignity, my self-respect, my self-esteem. I even lost my will to live. I almost lost my wife. We ended up in counseling, and I went to therapy. I finally realized that the only One who could salvage anything in my life was Christ. I turned to Him."

"How are you now?" I asked.

He said, "I have peace in my heart. I have peace of mind. I know that I'm growing. I'm learning a lot about what it means to have a relationship with the Lord. I know that I'm going to come through this time and that God has a future for me."

I believe that with and for this man. I believe that he is standing at the eight count and that the good fight of his faith is going to go on, and that in the not too distant future, he will not only have earned back everything that has been taken from him, but he will have even more—a newfound relationship with Jesus Christ. I believe he is on the rebound, ready to go for victory.

He's been down. But he's not out.

EXPECT A GOOD END TO THE FIGHT

When the late Dr. Norman Vincent Peale was visiting in our home a few years ago, I began telling him about all the problems I had as a school superintendent. I joked with him that it must be a lot easier to be a preacher who could travel from place to place rather than be a person who had a job that required he stay in one place and continually be faced with problem people and the problems they caused. I started to say, "Just try running a school system—"

He interrupted, "Billy, you've got a lot of problems?"

"About twenty-five of them," I said.

"Good, you've got a chance to grow and get strong in the Lord."

I said, "I never thought of it that way."

He said, "It's when you don't have any problems that you need to look up and say, 'Hey, what's wrong, Lord? Don't You trust me anymore?'"

Keep your reward in sight.

I said, "Well, God's got a *lot* of confidence in me."

We both enjoyed a good laugh, but the truth of what Dr. Peale said has stayed with me.

God knows you are taking a hit each time you are struck by a blow. If He doesn't step in to deliver you immediately, pause to consider the possibility that He is allowing you to take a hit for a reason—and that the reason is for your ultimate good.

The epistle of James begins with this teaching: "My brethren, count it all joy when you fall into various trials, knowing that the testing of your faith produces patience. But let patience have its perfect work, that you may be perfect and complete, lacking nothing" (1:2–4).

James doesn't say that faith will keep us from trials. Rather, trials will come, and faith allows us to work through those trials in such a way that something good comes from them.

If you've never had trials, these may sound like just so many words to you. But if you've been through trials, and if you've endured them with your faith intact, you know that these verses are true!

WHAT MIGHT BE THE REWARD?

The second thing you must think about is that if God has a reason for you to endure a hit, He must have a wonderful reward awaiting you. Throughout the New Testament, we find words of encouragement along these lines. We are told in Hebrews 11:6 that God is a "rewarder of those who diligently seek Him." We are told in 1 Corinthians 3:14: "If anyone's work which he has built on it endures, he will receive a reward." Jesus taught, "Your Father who sees in secret will Himself reward you openly" (Matt. 6:4).

The apostle Paul knew what it meant to take a hit for his faith. In defending his authority as an apostle, Paul told the Corinthians:

> From the Jews five times I received forty stripes minus one. Three times I was beaten with rods; once I was stoned; three times I was shipwrecked; a night and a day I have been in the deep; in journeys often, in perils of waters, in perils of robbers, in perils of my own countrymen, in perils of the Gentiles, in perils in the city, in perils in the wilderness, in perils in the sea, in perils among false brethren; in weariness and toil, in sleeplessness often, in hunger and thirst, in fastings often, in cold and nakedness—besides the other things, what comes upon me daily: my deep concern for all the churches (2 Cor. 11:24–28).

I find it difficult to imagine that a person could be more persecuted for his faith than Paul was and yet still stand on two feet. Paul knew what it meant to be in pain, to be in prison, and to face death because of his faith in Jesus Christ. And yet, he wrote to his beloved coworker Timothy, "I have fought the good fight, I have finished the race, I have kept the faith" (2 Tim. 4:7).

Part of what gives a boxer courage to get up and take

another hit is his hope of having his hand raised in triumph as the winner of the fight. Ultimately, every boxer dreams of a national or world championship.

For Paul, it was the hope of the Lord's reward that allowed him to take a hit. He also wrote to Timothy these words: "There is laid up for me the crown of righteousness, which the Lord, the righteous Judge, will give to me" (2 Tim. 4:8).

Keep your reward in sight. You may see stars when you take a hit, but put your focus on the stars that may be in your eternal crown!

BECOME AN OVERCOMER

Finally, keep in mind that nothing in this life guarantees that the good guys will win in this life. God's Word, however, promises that no good done by a person in this life will be overlooked and that the saints of God win in the life to come.

Some good people have suffered great losses.

Some fine people have been hit hard.

Some wonderful people have experienced terrible times.

Bad things do happen to good people. The church has had martyrs. And other religions have had them, too.

Nevertheless, good people outlast any bad that this life throws at them if they keep their faith in the Lord Jesus and endure to the end.

In the second and third chapters of the book of John's Revelation about Jesus Christ, we find repeated statements to the churches that are being judged. Each time we find words of great hope and encouragement being given to "him who overcomes." It is to the overcomers that the Lord makes these wonderful promises:

To him who overcomes I will give to eat from the tree of life, which is in the midst of the Paradise of God (2:7).

He who overcomes shall not be hurt by the second death (2:11).

To him who overcomes I will give some of the hidden manna to eat. And I will give him a white stone, and on the stone a new name written which no one knows except him who receives it (2:17).

He who overcomes, and keeps My works until the end, to him I will give power over the nations . . . and I will give him the morning star (2:26–28).

He who overcomes shall be clothed in white garments, and I will not blot out his name from the Book of Life; but I will confess his name before My Father and before His angels (3:5).

He who overcomes, I will make him a pillar in the temple of My God, and he shall go out no more. I will write on him the name of My God and the name of the city of My God, the New Jerusalem, which comes down out of heaven from My God. And I will write on him My new name (3:12).

To him who overcomes I will grant to sit with Me on My throne, as I also overcame and sat down with My Father on His throne (3:21).

Oh, there's a reward ahead! It's one worth taking a few hits for!

John later tells how the saints became overcomers. He said, "And they overcame him by the blood of the Lamb and by the word of their testimony, and they did not love their lives to the death" (Rev. 12:11).

We are to trust in what Jesus has done for us. We are to speak the truth about the Lord and about our relationship with Him. And we are to have courage.

We're called to be people capable of taking a hit, and yet staying in the fight, all the way to the final bell—no matter how big the giant that is thrown in the ring with us.

CHAPTER 18

Playing as Part of the Team

O ne morning in Parnell, which is a suburb of Auckland, New Zealand, I arose early enough to see the garbage being picked up. As the garbage truck came rumbling up Parnell Boulevard, two young men seemed to be running a relay with each other and the truck.

In front of each store was a round container that held a uniform-sized garbage can. One young man would pick up the full can and run it to the truck and empty it. The other one would run ahead to the next can and be waiting with it just as the truck got to him. Meanwhile, the first man ran the empty can back to the container and then jogged ahead to the next can along the road. They played leapfrog with the cans, and all the while, the truck never stopped moving. It just kept inching up the street.

I followed that truck for more than a half mile, and the two young men never missed a beat. They had their act together. They were a team.

All of us are a part of one team or another. Many of us play on several teams at one time—the family team, the team at work, the team at church, and so forth.

When we slay giants, we don't slay giants only for ourselves. We slay them for the people around us; we slay them for our team.

David didn't slay Goliath only for himself. He slew Goliath on behalf of all the Israelites and for the Israelites.

Caleb didn't slay the Anakim at Hebron only for himself. He claimed that territory for his family and all his descendants.

OUR OBLIGATION TO THE TEAM

As a former coach, I can tell you that the one player you don't want to have on your team is the lone star. This kid thinks that the team exists for him—that his teammates are on the field only to make him look good. Such a player, no matter how good he may be, kills team morale.

Take turns doing the hard tasks and difficult chores.

And who is it that every coach dreams of having? The truly talented player who doesn't have a big head about his ability and who encourages everybody else on the team to do the personal best. That kind of player is destined for greatness in the statistic books and for true leadership all through life.

We don't play the game of life on our own, although we may think we do. We can't do what we do without the help of a great many other people, some seen and some unseen. We are on a team whether we want to be or not. And as team members, we have obligations to the team.

Obligation #1: Do Your Part to Reach the Goal

Teams must have goals to stay together. Sometimes these goals aren't spoken, and when that happens, team members often get fuzzy about where the team is headed and why. If you don't know the goals of a particular team you are on—whether it's a civic organization or the work unit in which you function on the job—ask the team leader.

Make sure the goals are articulated. And more specifically, make sure your part on the team is articulated.

If you're going out with a team to slay a giant, know which giant you're going after and what job you have to play. Otherwise, things could get messy once the fighting begins.

Consider the way geese fly together. By instinct, they know which way they are headed—north in the spring, south in the fall. They fly in a V formation. The uplift created by each bird flapping its wings makes it easier for the birds behind it to fly. If a goose gets out of line, it immediately feels the resistance of the air. Over the long haul of a trip that is several hundred or even thousand miles long, this flight pattern allows the flock to add 70 percent to its flying range. Geese have discovered that when they share a common direction and work together, they achieve more and do so more efficiently. We human beings should be so smart!

Periodically, the lead bird slips back into a follow-up position. Another bird takes the lead, which is the position that requires the greatest strength. As birds move farther and farther back along the V, they find it easier and easier to fly. Eventually, each bird takes its turn in the difficult position of point-bird, and each bird also has a period of flying in the easier positions.

In life, we are wise to follow the same pattern. Take turns doing the hard tasks and difficult chores. When the time comes to rotate, rotate.

Which geese do the honking? The geese in the back of the V formation, not the lead goose. It's almost as if the geese in back are encouraging those ahead of them. Positive reinforcement always helps.

If one goose becomes sick and must drop out of the flight, two other geese will go down with it and stay with it to aid and protect it. When the time comes, they will fly on their own as a V of three, or they will join in with another group that comes flying overhead.

Teammates stick together. They help each other when the going gets tough.

Your part on the team may be to do the heavy work or to provide encouragement for those who do. Your part may be defense; it may be offense. Your part may be to lead; it may be to follow. Do your part. The team counts on it.

Obligation #2: Get Over the Loss

Even the best teams lose a game occasionally. That's life. Nobody has a perfect day every day.

When a loss occurs, the team must rebound immediately. The team that continues to focus on last Saturday's loss isn't going to be ready for next Saturday's game.

Individual players on a team sometimes give bad performances. When that happens, you need to do your best to encourage yourself and all of your teammates to shake the dust off the feet and start scrambling toward the next goal. If a player can't get over a loss, the entire team will suffer.

Companies lose bids. Thinking about the one that got away is a waste of time. Learn what you can from the experience, and go for the next project with gusto.

Families need to relocate. Dwelling on the neighbors and friends left behind only makes a move miserable. Start getting acquainted with people in your new town. Get involved and be active.

Churches have changes in leadership from time to time. Pining for the old pastor and the way things used to be done is counterproductive to spiritual growth. Dig in and make the most of the energy and ideas that a new leader has brought to your church.

Ben was one of my high school biology students. He had a very high IQ, but he did not do well in school. That may have been the result of his poor home life. Some people in our community called him a juvenile delinquent, even though he had never committed a crime.

Ben fell in love with Suzy, who was also in the biology class. She was the daughter of a friend of mine, a beautiful young girl, superlative in every way.

Ben and Suzy began to date, much to everybody's surprise.

After a few weeks, Suzy's family and friends apparently convinced her that she was going with the wrong kind of guy for her and she broke up with Ben. He was crushed and began acting out in very negative ways.

Finally, he came to talk to me. I invited Ben to go to church with me. A young couple in the church took him under their wing and invited him to several functions. Over the next few weeks and months, Ben began attending church regularly. He truly started to change in positive ways.

Suzy and Ben began dating again, and then, for reasons I don't know, Suzy again broke off their relationship.

Once again, Ben was devastated. This time, however, he didn't seek out a positive way of dealing with his hurt. He allowed himself to become **Teammates** extremely angry and bitter. As much as his friends **stick** and others tried to encourage him to go on with **together.** his life and find another girl to date, Ben held on to his hurt. He kept picking at his wounded heart until it festered and erupted into disaster.

Ben bought a magazine that explained how to rig a gift box with a gun so that the gun would go off when the person lifted the lid of the box. He made such a box and delivered it to Suzy's front porch. Fortunately, she opened the box from the side instead of the top, and the bullet from the gun hit her in the lower part of her body rather than her upper chest or head. She was badly wounded, but she lived.

For all his brilliance, Ben was ignorant. He not only lost any possibility of having a relationship with Suzy, but he lost the possibility of ever having any other girlfriend outside prison bars. Ben didn't have the ability to shake off the loss and get ready for the next day.

Three things happen when we dwell on past failures:

1. *Our anger grows until it becomes full-blown hatred.* We may start out not liking the fact that we lost the game, but we end up not liking the team that beat us, and eventually, we end up hating anybody associated with that team.

Don't allow yourself to personalize the anger you feel after a loss. See the loss as something that happened to you, and separate it from the person who may have inflicted the wounds, intentionally or unintentionally. In other words, separate the deed from the perpetrator as much as possible. This is especially true for an accident. A person can spend so much time and energy looking for a person to blame that she forestalls her healing process.

■ **Do your part.** ■ Learn from the loss. And if justice must be exacted from the one who inflicted the loss, let it be done through legal and moral channels. Don't take justice into your own hands. Once justice has been handed out, move on. Don't dwell on the hurt of the past.

2. *Hatred tends to create a pattern of revenge.* Revenge becomes a cycle with no end. When you strike out at a person or a group in revenge, they in turn strike back, and you strike yet again, and so forth. Family feuds and international conflicts have revenge at their root. Most of those who are in such feuds today can't even name what they initially fought over. They are so used to hating each other and seeking ways to do each other in, they have lost all sense of reason and logic. They are operating on gut-level hatred alone.

Avoid revenge. You can never exact it fully and completely. Revenge lies solely in God's domain. Only He can see the beginning from the ending. Only He knows exactly how to deal with sin, hate, and vengeful spirits.

3. *We become bitter as individuals.* Bitterness very often manifests itself in disease, loneliness, and inner anguish. Bitterness torments the soul. It infects everything and everyone it touches.

Never allow a loss to turn you into a bitter person. If it does, the person who beat you has beaten you twice—once directly and once indirectly.

Obligation #3: Stay Loyal to the Team

Don't leave your team because you have a bad game or because you lose a game. Stick with the team.

Too often spouses separate because they have gone through a tough time. Commit to each other to survive the tough time. Stay in the game. Nearly always, those who divorce have at least a few moments when they wish they hadn't. No marriage is perfect. You are only trading in one set of struggles for another.

The same holds for people who skip from one job to the next, looking for the ideal position and company. The perfect job doesn't exist. Each company has its own problems and benefits. Stay in the game. Fulfill your contract. Do your job.

How many people do you know who go from one church to the next, always leaving for what seems to be a legitimate reason? No church is perfect. Each has its flaws and problem people. Stay in the game. Keep your promises. Pay your pledges. Validate your vows. Be a faithful servant of the Lord, not one who flits from place to place.

Obligation #4: Play by the Team Rules

All teams have rules regarding team behavior. No coach lets his team members do whatever they want to do, whenever they want to do it, and then show up on Saturday to play. If a person is going to be a part of a team, he is going to have to show up for practices, follow instructions, eat the right things, do the full workout, and make the grades necessary. Team life is disciplined.

My commitment to do what was right as a coach was put to a severe test one year. It was midseason, and our team was undefeated. By virtue of our undefeated record, we were extended an invitation to represent the nine high schools in our city against the best team in the county. The tournament was the Jefferson County Classic.

The team, student body, parents, teachers—in fact, the entire community—were excited about our participation in this tournament. We were predicted to win, and we were confident.

Prior to the beginning of the tournament, we had a regularly scheduled game against a team in Bessemer, Alabama, that was mediocre at best. My primary challenge as a coach was to prevent my players from becoming overconfident.

We made the twenty-two-mile trip to Bessemer by private automobiles. I took four players with me, another parent drove four players, and I allowed one player to drive his own car and take three of this teammates. We arrived enthusiastic, ready to win.

My enthusiasm was quickly dashed when a parent approached me with some "news I should hear." This father proceeded to tell me that he had passed the car driven by one of the players and had noticed the athletes inside it were smoking. He reminded me that I had a strict team policy against smoking or drinking alcoholic beverages. It was a well-known fact that violation of the policy would result in dismissal from the team. The father wanted to know what I was going to do about the matter.

I must admit that my first thought was, *Why did this man choose this time to bring this matter to my attention?* I didn't have to go far for the answer. His son was a substitute player on the team, and he perhaps believed there was a chance for his son to become a starter if some of the first-string players were dismissed. I was angry with him for having such a motive, but even more disappointed in my players.

I went back to the dressing room and asked the players if the allegations were true. Without blinking an eye, the four starters accused stepped forward and said, "It's true, Coach. We're sorry. We had one cigarette, and we passed it around. It was stupid of us to do it."

I was heartened by their courage to admit the wrongdoing and by their obvious disappointment in themselves. At the same time, I had no choice but to follow team policy. I thanked them for their honesty and instructed them to take off their uniforms and turn them in to the team manager. We began warm-ups with eight players instead of twelve. The crowd began buzzing. Soon the word was out that four starters had violated team policy and were off the team.

The team struggled. By halftime we were behind. As I

headed for the dressing room, I was approached by parents who tried to convince me that the four players should be allowed to return to the team. I didn't back down, and we lost the game, even though our eight players had played hard.

Back at school, I took the opportunity to give the entire team some advice. I said, "Do what is right. The consequences of poor decisions can be severe."

I faced intense opposition that winter. Parents, school officials, and booster club enthusiasts were all opposed to the action I had taken. Still, I knew it was the right thing to do—right for the team and, ultimately, right for the four boys.

Fortunately, all four players who were dismissed from the team were juniors and could try out for the team the following year as seniors, which they did. They had an outstanding year, with exemplary behavior, and they won the Big Nine Championship.

> ■ **We are our brother's keeper.** ■

The boys told me that if they had been allowed to come back on the team after their offense as juniors, they never would have developed the attitude and discipline that made them champions during their senior year. Knowing that their behavior had consequences made them all the more determined to exhibit good behavior and to show what they were truly capable of doing—both in competition and in life.

Every team has rules. Play by them. The discipline of obedience will stand you in good stead when you face individual giants, and the discipline will be a must when you face team giants.

Obligation #5: Uphold Your Team Honor

Uphold your team honor even when you are out of uniform and off the field.

Be faithful to your spouse when you are away from home. Speak well of your company when you are away from the office or factory. Encourage others to attend your church if they don't have a church home, and speak well of those who worship with you.

In running down your team, you run down yourself.

At times, we need to recognize that we are required to do what is right for the team, even if it causes us a few uneasy moments. As individuals who call ourselves Christians, we have an obligation to the entire team known as the church. We bear the name of Christ twenty-four hours a day, not just when we sit in a pew. We are members of the Lord's team wherever we go.

This lesson came home to me a few months ago. I boarded a plane, knowing that I had two flights ahead of me before I arrived in a fairly small town where I was to meet a colleague for a business meeting. Even as I was flying to our destination, the colleague was driving from another direction. Both of us were leaving about the same time.

No sooner had we all prepared for takeoff than the announcement was made that a part on one of the wheels of the plane needed to be replaced. The part had been ordered, but we were going to have a significant delay. A number of us deplaned while the repair was made. I began to explore travel alternatives—such as other flights, a rental car, and so forth. The ticket agent assured me that I would still be able to make my connecting flight, but that I would have only a few minutes to get from one gate to the next. Her final words were, "If you take off by 12:35, you'll make it. Otherwise, it will be several hours until the next flight."

We were called to reboard the flight at 12:20. I sighed a big sigh of relief and thought, *That's a prayer answered.* I noticed that the woman across the aisle from me had not returned. She had made a couple of trips in and out of the plane, and her purse and carry-on luggage were still under the seat. At 12:30, the doors of the plane were closed, and we began to pull away.

I faced a major dilemma. Should I alert the flight crew to the missing passenger and cause a delay that would mean the possibility of my missing my connecting flight and, in so doing, missing an important business meeting? Or should I speak up?

I could have taken the viewpoint, *It's her fault. She should have been back on the plane. I'm not her keeper.*

But the fact is, we *are* our brother's keeper. That argument didn't convince the Lord the first time it was used, and it hasn't convinced Him since.

I called to the flight attendant and told her that the passenger across the aisle was still in the terminal. The flight attendant went immediately to the captain, and the captain and the control tower conversed for a few minutes. We then returned to the gate, picked the woman up, and taxied back out to the runway where we had to wait in line once again. Precious minutes were ticking by.

When the woman reboarded the plane, the flight attendant said, "You need to thank that man for your being on this plane." She just laughed, trying to justify her delay by saying that she was on the phone. The man next to me said, "We should have left her."

No. The right thing had been done. It didn't matter ultimately that we took off late. It didn't matter that she was oblivious to the trouble she had caused, or that she was ungrateful. What mattered was that a right choice had been made. One small insignificant act—and yet it may have been the most important thing I did that day in forming my character as a human being, and in becoming more equipped for what the Lord has ahead for me both now and in eternity. (By the way, I did make my connection.)

We don't know which choices in life are the big ones and which ones are inconsequential. Every choice and decision we make is a potential life changer, and certainly a life developer. When we see ourselves as *always* being part of the Lord's team, we live as a team player at all times, in all situations.

THE LORD KNOWS ABOUT THE GIANTS

In the end, we must come to the fact that the Lord knows about the giants. He knows where they are, who they are, what they are, and how they can be defeated. More than our defeating giants, however, we are to become giant slayers in the inner being. Each of us is to have the character of a giant slayer.

When we come to the final days of our lives, many things won't matter. What will matter is who we have become. What will matter is the state of the soul.

John Luther once said, "Good character is more to be praised than outstanding talent. Most talents are, to some extent, a gift. Good character, by contrast, is not given to us. We have to build it piece by piece—by thought, choice, courage, and determination."

The choices we make nearly always affect other people. In fact, it's difficult to make a choice that doesn't touch another person's life in some way.

Keep your team in mind when you make life's choices, and ultimately, keep in mind our Team Leader, the Lord Himself. He is the One who makes the team rules. He is the One who lines up our opponents and sets the schedule and gives us our dreams and desires. He is the One who organizes the members of the team and asks that we be loyal to them and to Him. He is the One who will evaluate our performance.

You can't be loyal to a team without being loyal to the Coach, and you can't be loyal to the Coach without being loyal to His team.

CHAPTER 19

Inspiring
Giant-Slaying
Thinking
in Others

I n the fall of 1957, I was both excited and frightened. An impossible dream had come true for me.
I had graduated from Birmingham Southern College and had been hired as a teacher and coach at West End
High School in Birmingham, Alabama.

West End High was my alma mater. I had received my
high school diploma from there in 1951. After serving in the
military, working in a steel mill, and going to college, I was
back at my old school, determined to succeed and scared at
the same time. Each day was a new challenge.

One of my professors at Birmingham Southern College—
a man who was also the athletic director at the college—lived
in West End, and he had a son, Billy, who attended West
End High. Billy wanted to be a football player.

The only problem was that Billy was a short overweight
kid who lacked any physical resemblance to a football player.
Every day the coaches would shift him from one position to
another to try to find a slot for him, although none of the
coaches thought he had much of a chance of making a positive contribution to the team. He was the slowest kid on the
team, and he quickly acquired the nickname Turtle.

One day as Billy's father and I were visiting, he said, "I

don't want to tell you how to coach, but I would like to share with you something that I believe is very important. The word *education* comes from the Latin word *educere*. It means to 'draw out the best of others; to help one develop his potential.'"

I listened carefully, wondering where the conversation was going. Billy's father continued, "My son, Billy, is only thirteen, and I will agree with you that he doesn't look much like a football player today. However, the important thing is that we not see Billy as he is today, but see him as he can be four years from now. It's easy to look at a freshman and see him as he is with all of his inadequacies and limitations and not be too excited about his ability to contribute to the team. Let's try to see Billy as he can be as a senior. What might he be like in four years, with a lot of guidance, coaching, and physical growth? I try to see my son as he will look physically by the time he's sixteen or seventeen. I predict he will weigh between 185 and 190 pounds and be six one or six two in height. Coach, can you see Billy with an all-American jersey covering his broad shoulders and narrow waist?"

I must confess, I had never imagined Billy that way. In fact, if I was honest, I'd have to admit that at that time, I didn't have an ability to see anyone, including myself, as the person might be in the future. I still had a certain degree of grasshopper mentality that kept me locked in the present and past.

Those few minutes with Coach Battle made a positive imprint on my life, one that made me a better teacher, coach, principal, superintendent of schools, husband, father, and grandfather. I learned to see people as they might be, not as they were or are. I began to see people's strengths rather than focus on their weaknesses. I began to emphasize the positive rather than the negative.

Billy was one of the most dedicated kids I ever coached. He knew what it meant to pay the price and go the second mile. I spent many an hour throwing a football to him as he matured. I took extra time to teach him the fundamentals of football and to use his hands effectively as a football player. I started seeing him in my mind's eye as a future all-American.

By the time Billy was a senior, he was six two and weighed 188 pounds. He had big, broad shoulders and a very small waistline. His physical stature was the same as the picture his father had painted for me of Billy four years earlier. At the conclusion of his senior season, I saw the young man put on an all-American jersey and participate in an all-American high school game. The picture of Billy that Coach Battle helped me to envision had become a reality.

■ *How do you see others today?* ■

Billy Battle went to the University of Alabama on a football scholarship. While at Alabama, he played on a national championship team and had the privilege of playing in the Sugar, Orange, and Cotton Bowls.

At the age of twenty-eight, Billy Battle became the youngest head coach in the nation when he took a job at the University of Tennessee. He later left coaching with a winning percentage of more than 800 percent. Not bad for a young kid who was overweight and so slow that his teammates called him Turtle.

How do you see others today? Your children? Your grandchildren? The students you teach? The young men and women you coach?

How do you see your employees, your peers, your friends?

Do you see them as winners or as grasshoppers in the land of giants?

WE LEAVE AN IMPRINT

Whether we want to or not, whether we mean to or not, whether we think about it or not, we leave an imprint on every person we meet. In some way, the imprint on that person will help him become a giant slayer or a person with grasshopper mentality.

Several people in my life helped imprint me with giant-slaying thinking. Each of these people helped me in a distinct way.

Katherine Baker has been my mother-in-law for more than forty years. In the early years of my marriage to Carolyn, she fed us many a meal to help us make ends meet. She helped us survive financially, but even more important, she encouraged me to pursue my dreams. She repeatedly told me, "You can be anything you want to be, Billy. Your work habits and desire will take you a long way." She encouraged me to set my sights high and not doubt myself.

I learned from my mother-in-law the value of having someone encourage you day in and day out, focusing on your strengths and believing in your best.

Another person who made a positive imprint on me was Harry Earl McNeil, one of my college professors at Birmingham Southern. I was not the least bit interested in taking college preparatory courses in high school, and as a result, when I entered college, I wasn't the least bit prepared for taking a course such as a foreign language. When I learned that I had to have two years of foreign language to graduate, I nearly panicked. I didn't see how I could ever hurdle this barrier.

Through my involvement with the Baptist Student Union, I met Professor McNeil. He was the faculty sponsor for the BSU, and we came to respect each other a great deal. He admired my stance against alcoholic beverages and my devotion to my wife and son. I respected his boldness in standing up for God.

Professor McNeil became Señor McNeil, my Spanish professor. As I had expected, I struggled in his class. He kept telling me not to be afraid of being successful in Spanish, but I was too filled with grasshopper mentality at the time to believe him.

It wasn't something that Señor McNeil said, but something that he *did* that turned the tide for me. He invited me to come to his house every Thursday evening to eat pancakes and study Spanish. I spent Thursday nights in his home for two years, and in the process, I learned Spanish and passed the required courses. We also built up the attendance of the Baptist Student Union in those two years. We enjoyed a win-win relationship.

Señor McNeil taught me the great value of going a second mile in getting a person to believe he can slay a giant.

Robert Lacey encouraged me to join the ROTC, which I did. He also got me interested in boxing and helped me to become a Golden Glove champion. He continually reminded me that it's not who you are that's important, but who you think you are. If you think you're somebody special, you will be. If you think you're a nobody, you'll wind up a nobody. He frequently reminded me that growing up in a federal housing project didn't make a person a nobody, but that thinking you were a nobody would.

Robert Lacey was a steady reminder that your past doesn't need to be your future.

Tilford Junkins was my childhood pastor. He taught me at an early age the importance of loving Jesus and being committed to the things you believe in. It was largely because of his influence in my life that during my years of military service, I carried a New Testament in my fatigue jacket pocket and read it every day. Later, he performed my wedding ceremony. Tilford Junkins was a tough, tell-it-like-it-is preacher who never censored the teaching of God's Word to gain people's approval. He was a man's man, and he taught me that a person could be a tough giant slayer and still be a nice person and a believer in Christ Jesus.

Ken Blanchard, coauthor of *The One-Minute Manager,* has made a positive imprint on my life. He instilled a desire in me to want to be nice to people every day. He lives this principle daily as well or better than anybody I have ever known. I greatly admire his generosity, which manifests itself in some wonderful treats for people. I'll never forget the time when Ken invited Carolyn and me to his home in California. We were to go from his home to tape a one-hour television program for CNN, and Ken said he'd arrange transportation for us. He surely did! A big stretch limo showed up, and the chauffeur drove us up to Beverly Hills and then back to his home after the taping. Carolyn and I had been in a limousine before, but not for a 150-mile trip. I have no doubt that we walked a little taller and had an extra dose of confidence as we stepped from that limo to do the program.

Ken is the classic example in my life of a person who goes above and beyond. And he never seems to think that he is doing anything special. A lot of people keep score when they compliment or encourage others. Ken never does.

Many teachers encouraged me to graduate from high school, something nobody else in my family had done. All of them were people with whom I have or have had fairly long-standing relationships. They were encouragers to me, people who believed in my ability to become a giant slayer. They represent to me the best ideals of what is required to instill a giant-slaying attitude into someone else:

- Offering steady encouragement, believing in a person's potential and good qualities to take her to success
- Putting words to actions and helping a person walk the walk toward success
- Encouraging a person to look beyond his past to the dreams he can have, and realize, in his future
- Modeling behavior that a giant slayer can be and should be a person of high moral standards with faith in God
- Giving something extra to somebody else, and never expecting anything in return

Another man came into my life at just the opportune moment with just the right words. He represents to me the influence a person can have even if he doesn't know the other person well.

That man was Bill Burch. But to tell about his impact on my life, I need to give you a little background.

MY DREAM OF BEING A TEACHER
AND A COACH

After high school, I joined the military. In fact, I left for the army two hours after my high school graduation ceremony. I had never expected to receive a high school diploma, and quite frankly, I was surprised that I was receiving one!

When I came back from military service, I went to work in a steel mill. All the members of my family worked in the steel mills.

While I was working at the steel mill, my thoughts turned increasingly to the people who had been a source of encouragement to me when I was in high school. I thought about the teachers and coaches who had enabled me to graduate. They grew large in my thinking. They were my true heroes. For fifteen months, I nurtured a dream of being like them. And even though I knew nothing about what it meant to get into a college, much less what might be involved in graduating from college, I knew that if I was to realize my dream, I would need a college education.

I finally got up enough nerve to go to a college in the city where I was working and to make an appointment with a counselor to inquire about admission. The counselor quickly reviewed my high school record, and after about fifteen minutes of meeting with me, he concluded, "Son, there's nothing in your past that would indicate that you could ever be successful in college. You have a good job in the steel mill, and you are making good money. My advice to you is that you stay there."

I walked out of that man's office in a daze. I had been a championship boxer and knew how to take a hit, but not a hit like that. I sat down on the curb, wiped the tears that began springing from my eyes, and faced the possibility that I might never become a teacher or a coach. That was a painful idea, and as is so often the case, one painful idea triggered another.

I thought back through all of the disappointments I had

known in my life. My mother and father divorced when I was a young child, and in the wake of that, disappointment had figured largely in my life.

I knew what it meant not to see a father. The last memory I have of my father was when I was four. I remember only that he gave me a quarter to buy a candy bar and a soft drink in a downtown hotel.

I knew what it meant to be the only child in my first grade class who had a last name that was different from the name of his mother.

You have the chance for something better.

I knew what it meant to have teachers buy my books and pencils and even my shoes because we were too poor to buy those necessities.

I knew what it was to have an absentee mother. My mother traveled with my stepfather, who was in the navy, and my brother, sister, and I grew up at my grandmother's home.

I knew what it meant to receive only a couple of oranges in my stocking at Christmas, while other children received toys and new clothes.

All of those memories came flooding back as I sat on that curb. The counselor had unleashed the locked-up negatives in my life, and as I got in my car and headed back to the plant, I felt enveloped by a fog of discouragement and despair.

Have you ever been in fog? It disorients you and causes you to see things around you in a little different way—if you are able to see things at all. I thought I was headed back to the steel mill, where I worked the three to eleven shift, but in my mental fog, I took a wrong turn. A few minutes later, I saw a sign that read "Birmingham Southern College." I drove to the top of the hill without thinking about what I was doing, found a parking place, and parked my car. I got out and stood by my car, trying to regain my composure. Nobody knew what I was thinking or where I had planned to go that day, and I didn't want anybody to see me in such a discouraged state.

Before I fully knew what was happening, a tall gentleman with a big smile on his face walked up, stuck his hand out toward me, and introduced himself as Bill Burch, coach at Birmingham Southern. He asked me if I was a new student, and I told him no. I then told him that I didn't think I was ever going to be a student at any college, and I relayed to him how the counselor at the other college had told me that my past would most likely keep me from ever being successful in college.

He quickly said, "Son, listen to me. There are a lot of people in this world who will tell you what you *can't* do. Never listen to them. Listen to the people who tell you what you *can* do."

I shared with him my desire to be a coach and teacher. He said, "You want to be a coach and teacher? Is that really what you want to do with your life?"

I said, "Yes, sir."

He said, "Would you like to go to college here?"

At that point, I would have been eager to go to college anywhere, but to go to a college where a near total stranger had faith I could get in and succeed seemed inviting. I replied that I would. With that, he escorted me to the admissions office, and with his assistance and encouragement, I enrolled in Birmingham Southern. I later discovered it was one of the top ten liberal arts colleges in the nation at that time. Coach Burch and the admissions counselors assured me that I could get into the married couples housing on campus. The rent was twenty-five dollars a month. I knew I could handle that with what I earned at my job.

I drove down that hill elated, without a trace of mental fog and not a bit of discouragement. I was going to be a college student!

I drove straight to the steel mill and asked my boss, Mr. McClellan, if I could work the 11:00 P.M. to 7:00 A.M. shift for six months. I'm not sure that anyone had ever volunteered for the graveyard shift before. He asked me why I wanted to work nights, and I told him that I was going to attend college in the daytime. He granted my wish, even though he doubted I would be able to work all night, go to school, and be successful at either my job or my studies. He didn't know how determined I was.

In a period of one-half day, I met one of the most discouraging people in my life. I left his office feeling lower than a grasshopper, facing a giant that was taller than any giant in Canaan. He had conveyed to me one of the main traits of grasshopper thinking: *your past determines your future.* That same afternoon, I met one of the most encouraging people in my life. He had conveyed to me one of the main traits of thinking like a winner in the land of giants: *you have a chance for something better.*

Every day, we meet people who need our encouraging words to believe for their highest potential and best future. In many cases, we don't know these people, and we may never see them again. That doesn't mean that the role as an encourager is diminished. Bill Burch crossed my path at a pivotal moment. My entire future changed in a matter of a couple of hours because he chose to greet me with a smile and to stop for a few minutes of positive conversation that made me believe again that I could be a winner in the land of giants.

GIANT-SLAYING PRINCIPLES TO PASS ON

As you encounter your loved ones, family members, and even strangers, keep these six principles in mind. They can help another person see herself as a giant slayer.

Principle #1: A Person Is Never Too Young or Too Old to Be a Giant Slayer

Giant-slaying thinking doesn't come with maturity. Children can be victims of grasshopper mentality, and grandparents can, too. Or children can see themselves as giant slayers, and so can older people.

Benjamin Franklin was a newspaper columnist at sixteen, and a signer of the Constitution when he was eighty-one.

Ted Williams, at age forty-two, hit a home run in his last official time at bat. Mickey Mantle, on the other hand, was only twenty when he hit twenty-three home runs in his first full year as a major-league player.

Golda Meir was seventy-one when she became prime minister of Israel. William Pitt II was twenty-four when he became prime minister of England.

■ *We need to become good finders.* ■

Mozart was only seven years old when his first composition was published. George Bernard Shaw was ninety-four when one of his plays was first performed.

Age has little relationship to your ability to see yourself as a success and maximize your potential.

Principle #2: To Think of Himself as a Giant Slayer, a Person Must First Accept His Uniqueness as an Individual

Help people discover what they can do best, what they desire to do, and what they are willing to work hard at accomplishing. See each person as an individual, and help the person see himself the same way.

The late Coach Paul "Bear" Bryant said in an interview with Dick Cavett that he never treated all of his players alike. Rather, he treated them all fairly. His approach was that all players should be treated uniquely because all players were different as individuals. Bryant said, "I coach people. Assistant coaches coach football."

Coach Bryant no doubt held that position, in part, because of the way he saw himself. When he died in 1983, a story in *Time* magazine said of him, "He knew who he was." The magazine quoted the Bear himself as saying, "God did give me the gift of leading men. I can do that."

We all have the tendency to look longingly at the achievements of others. We wonder what it might be like to be a bank vice president, to start our own business, to be a concert violinist, to host a talk show, to bake a prize-winning cake. Rather, we must turn our eyes toward ourselves and ask, What did God give me the ability to do? When we concentrate on our uniqueness, we find our success.

Principle #3: Never Typecast Another Person by Her Outward Appearance or the Environment in Which She Grew Up

A teacher told me when I was just a child, "You'll never amount to a hill of beans." I had been sitting in a group of children who were talking, and I had not been misbehaving. By that time, a grasshopper mentality was deeply rooted in me, and I never would have given a teacher cause to notice me, much less to punish me. Yet, she had singled me out for that comment.

Why? In retrospect I believe it was solely a result of the way I was dressed. I was living in a low-cost federal housing project at the time—Elyton Village. In today's terms, it was a ghetto. The children of that project went to school in a well-to-do middle-class neighborhood. Our clothes, which generally were not as nice as those of our peers, and the rough spots of our behavior set us apart as village kids.

Her comment was mainly about my *environment,* not about me personally. Still, she had transferred her opinion about my circumstances to me. And as a young child, I took what she said at face value: *I wouldn't amount to a hill of beans.*

She didn't say, "You won't amount to a hill of beans *unless . . .*"

She didn't say, "You're going to need to work hard to overcome your past and really make something of yourself, but I believe you can do it."

She didn't say, "You have had a rough beginning, but your beginning doesn't need to be your ending."

No. She made a blanket statement about my past, present, and future. And as a young child hearing that from the mouth of an authority figure, I took what she said as a statement of fact, not opinion.

To convey giant-slaying thinking to a person, you need to look into her potential and truly see her as a person created by God, destined for a purpose planned by God, and capable of being filled with God's Spirit to accomplish her purpose in life. To help another person think like a giant slayer, encourage her to see herself as God sees her: loved, equipped, and blessed.

Principle #4: Look for the Good and Praise It

We need to become "good finders." When we look for and find good in someone, we need to call attention to it. We begin by finding the small ordinary good things of each day.

Unfortunately, we often neglect to praise the good we see in those with whom we live. When people do something that we appreciate or value, we need to let them know it.

I learned this some time ago in my relationship with my wife, Carolyn. For many years I have had a habit of getting up early in the morning, going for a good fast run in my neighborhood, returning home for a shower and change of clothes, and then sitting down for breakfast before going to work.

My favorite breakfast is homemade biscuits and milk gravy, southern style. Carolyn bakes the best biscuits in the world, and I have been enjoying her delicious biscuits every morning for years. One morning, I sat down to breakfast and noticed that instead of biscuits, toast was on my plate. Carolyn had put a toaster right on the table and had made whole wheat toast for me instead of my usual biscuits and gravy.

I assumed that she didn't have the ingredients she needed to make biscuits that morning. I didn't think any more about it until the next morning when I had another breakfast of whole wheat toast. This routine continued about a week. Finally, I asked Carolyn if she would like for me to go to the store and buy the ingredients she needed to make biscuits.

"I have what I need for biscuits," she said. "I just thought I would make toast instead."

"Why?" I asked in an aggrieved voice. "You know how much I enjoy your biscuits and gravy."

"Well, no," Carolyn replied. "I actually didn't know you cared about my biscuits one way or another. You have never said anything."

I got the message. I spent the next few minutes telling her in some detail how much her biscuits meant to me. The next morning, I found biscuits and gravy on the breakfast table again. I didn't miss my cue. "Thanks for these biscuits," I said. "These are really great!" And I meant every word of it.

As an educator, I was taught years ago about the value of positive reinforcement—of calling attention to the positive and praising it. It's a principle that works not only in the classroom but in every area of life.

Principle #5: Giant-Slaying Thinking Can Begin in a Moment, but It Develops Over Time

Don't expect giant-slaying thinking to take hold in another person's life overnight.

Consider the example of the Chinese bamboo tree. If you were to plant the seedling of a Chinese bamboo tree and water and nurture it consistently, you might quickly become discouraged unless you knew about the growth cycle of that particular plant. There is no visible growth of a Chinese bamboo seedling the first year, the second year, the third year, or the fourth year. But during the fifth year, look out! The tree will grow nearly ninety feet in six weeks. Some people claim that if you stand next to a Chinese bamboo plant as it is growing, you can hear it snap, crackle, and pop.

Does the Chinese bamboo actually lie dormant for five years waiting to grow? Not at all. During the first four years, the tree is putting down and developing a strong root system that can accommodate the tremendous visible vertical growth the fifth year. Without that root system in place, the stalk above ground would topple over quickly. In fact, such growth would not be possible without the massive nurturing from the roots.

Instilling positive thoughts and values into another person's life is like nurturing a Chinese bamboo seedling. We must stay after it and be steady in our words and behavior day in and day out, year in and year out. Growth will eventually manifest itself.

Principle #6: Help the Person Achieve His Best Without Criticizing Him for Failing to Achieve Your Definition of Best

Not long ago, I saw a man I hadn't seen in a number of years. We had been in Rotary Club together, and he went on to tell me some of the local news, including the death of the son of a man we both had known.

The young man, an outstanding student, had brought home his first B ever on a report card. His mother was so upset at seeing the B that she called his father at work, and the father also became very upset. The parents couldn't believe their son had earned a B! The father told the boy that he could no longer play basketball or be active in other extracurricular activities until he got that B back up to an A. The parents were extremely disappointed that their son had earned a B.

No doubt feeling himself to be a failure, the sixteen-year-old shot himself. His suicide stunned the community and truly devastated his parents.

Shortly after Carolyn and I heard that story, our granddaughter brought home her report card, and we were surprised to see that she had received a C in reading. We asked her whether she knew why she had earned a C or whether she had experienced a problem in reading at school. Michelle responded that she didn't know.

In our opinion, our granddaughter is a fine young reader for her age, so we suggested to her and to her parents that they ask the teacher what the problem seemed to be so that we all could help her in that area. At no time, however, did we register disappointment in Michelle or think in terms of punishment. We talked in terms of what the problem might be so that it could be overcome.

The next day, Michelle went to school, and her teacher said, "I made one of the biggest mistakes of my life, Michelle. I put down the wrong grade for you in reading. Your actual grade is a B + ." She sent a letter home to Michelle's parents, apologizing. In the letter, she also noted that Michelle was one of the best readers in her class. What a pleasant surprise the letter was—something you read about but never expect to happen to you!

How many times have we seen parents at a Little League game expect their children to get a hit each time they come to bat?

How many supervisors expect every employee to do a perfect job every time?

How many teachers expect all of their students to get top marks?

We all are guilty at times of wanting another person to achieve at a level that *we* have selected rather than be content to encourage him to do *his* best. Helping another person be a winner in the land of giants requires that we help her identify *her* dreams, set *her* goals, make *her* plans, and defeat *her* giants.

CHAPTER 20

Stirring the Nest

An eagle has an interesting life cycle. When the time comes for a mother eagle to lay her eggs, she locates a spot high on a mountain. She then selects sticks, branches, briars, and even small limbs to make the superstructure of the nest, which must not only be able to stand the high-mountain winds but also the weight of her brood. Finally, she gathers soft materials such as leaves, grass, rabbit skins, and even down from her own body to make the nest soft for the eaglets.

After the eaglets hatch, the mother eagle spends all of her time meeting their needs for food. The eaglets grow rapidly, and soon, they nearly crowd each other out of the nest.

Eventually, the day comes when the mother eagle knows that it is time for her eaglets to begin to fly. She does two things. First, she stops feeding them. She returns home from her hunting expeditions without food for them. You can almost imagine the young eagles turning to one another and asking, "What's with Mom today?"

Next, she begins to break apart the nest. With her sharp beak, she starts taking out the soft lining of the nest, leaving the prickly briars and sticks. By this time the eaglets are flapping in protest. Their mom has a strange gleam in her eye for sure!

The mother eagle continues to stir the nest. From the eaglets' perspective, she may seem to be uncaring, unloving. From her perspective, she is pushing her offspring toward the destiny for which they were created—to soar the heavens as eagles. She is preparing her brood for bigger and better things.

In teaching her eaglets how to fly, the mother eagle flutters over her young like a helicopter. She is giving them a lesson about the power and capability of their wings.

We learn from taking tests.

- She then sits on the edge of the nest, sticking her beak into the air. As an updraft rises from the valley below, it ruffles her feathers, and she suddenly hurls herself into the midst of the wind, catching the draft in her wings and soar-
- ing out over the valley below. She is showing her eaglets how to catch and ride the wind.

In hovering and hurling, the mother eagle is giving her offspring a lesson in aerodynamics. No other birds have such powerful, massive wings. No other large birds can hover as they can or fly higher. The mother eagle is teaching her brood that the wind is their friend and they must learn to master the air currents. But to the eaglets, it's a giant world outside the nest!

Finally, the mother eagle carries an eaglet on her wings and off they fly. Suddenly, the mother eagle swoops down and flings her eaglet in her wake. It's time to fly! It's time for the young eagle to soar on its own.

The Scriptures tell us that the Lord carries us as if we are on eagle's wings. He desires for us to soar—to fulfill our destinies. He desires for us to be more than conquerors, to be mighty men and women of valor, to be victorious in thought, word, and deed—both in the inner person and in outer achievements.

WHO ALLOWS THE GIANT TO EXIST?

I'm certainly not one to advocate that all of the giants we face in our lives are sent by God. Some of them are of our own creation as I have pointed out in previous chapters. Others are tricks and ploys of the Enemy of the soul, who comes at us stalking and roaring like a lion. But sometimes, giants that cross our paths are tests sent by God.

As a teacher, I frequently gave tests—from quizzes to final exams. My giving tests didn't have anything to do with whether I liked my students or not.

I didn't give tests to set up my students for failure or to destroy their egos, although I'm sure a few students took it that way.

No, I gave tests so that my students could see how much of a certain body of information they had learned and, at the same time, gain an awareness of what they needed to master. In taking a test, students have an opportunity to discover what they know and what they don't know.

We learn from taking tests. In many cases, we learn what we didn't know, and we learn the right answers to the missed questions. There is great value in that.

Life's tests are much the same way. God doesn't give them to us to punish us or to destroy us. He doesn't give them to us because He no longer loves us. On the contrary, He gives us tests so that we can see how much we have grown in Him and how much we still need to grow.

Without tests, we very often are content to sit in the soft and lofty eagle's nest and watch life go by. Without tests, we never try our wings. Without tests, we don't really know who we are, what we are capable of doing, or why God put us on this earth. Through life's tests, and very often from our mistakes, we find out what we are made of and what we are destined to do.

Tests also reveal to us the strength of our faith.

When the disciples found themselves in a storm on the Sea of Galilee, Jesus asked them, "Where is your faith?" At other times, He said to them, "O you of little faith." He was pointing out to them that they were supposed to use their faith to meet needs and solve problems. They were supposed to grow in faith and become strong in faith. Jesus was giving them tests to prepare them for the day when He would no longer be with them in the flesh.

Some of the giants today are ones we will defeat readily. We can rejoice when we do so that our faith has become stronger than it once was.

Some of the giants will deal blows to us. We can also rejoice when that happens. We are learning that our faith isn't yet as strong as it can be, and will be, if we will continue to exercise our faith and stay obedient to the Lord.

IS GOD STIRRING YOUR NEST?

Sometimes the Lord is stirring our nest to take a step forward in our lives, to grow up in an area where we need to grow up, to take on the new project that is right for us to pursue. Sometimes the Lord is giving us a giant of an opportunity!

Sometimes the Lord stirs our nest with conviction, letting us become miserable in the habit that needs to be changed or the problem that needs to be confronted until we reach the point where we are willing to make important changes in our lives.

Perhaps the greatest stirring of a nest comes when the Holy Spirit begins to hover over us and convict us of our sinful natures. Sin in our lives is the biggest giant we will ever face. At some point in our lives, we are forced to face the fact that we are sinners, separated from God by our sin, and that we are in danger of God's judgment.

A few years ago, I came across a term in my experience as an investor and businessman that I had never read before: *judgment proof.*

I went to the library and read everything I could about being judgment proof. In business terms, this phrase is used in contracts so that a person can't be held liable for any losses should a venture fail. The person who shrewdly declares himself contractually to be judgment proof has protection against creditors who may want to come after his assets.

Until that day, the thought of becoming judgment proof had never entered my mind. And yet the more I thought about that phrase, the more appropriate it seemed to me—not in a business sense, but in a spiritual sense. How important it is that we become judgment proof regarding the consequences associated with our sins!

In my life, the conviction that I needed to face the true nature of my relationship with God started to come home on a hot September afternoon in the early 1960s on the West End High School football practice field.

Football practice had ended with the usual sprints of twenty, fifty, seventy-five, and a hundred yards. We had been through a very good practice, considering the heat and humidity. A few tempers had flared every now and then, and a couple of players had engaged in brief skirmishes. That was not unusual, either. Overall, the goals for our practice had been achieved, and the players and coaches alike felt good about the upcoming game two nights away.

> **Sometimes the Lord is giving us a giant of an opportunity.**

As I started toward the gym to shower, dress, and go home to spend some time with my wife and two sons, one of the players fell into stride with me. Holding his helmet under his left arm, he said, "Coach, mind if I walk with you to the gym?"

"Not at all," I replied.

Then Harold shocked me with these words: "Coach, I want to thank you for your Christian influence. It's great to have a coach like you who believes in the Lord and expects the best out of you. You know, Coach, every day we go out and practice the skills and attitudes that we must have in order to become a winner, on and off the field. Thanks for being a positive influence in our lives and preparing us to be successful. I think I would like to become a coach one day and help build young men and see them grow mentally and physically. That's a big responsibility, though. The influence that coaches have on the lives of others is staggering."

As we neared the gym door, he said these words that still ring in my mind today, some thirty years later. He said, "Coach, thanks for making your influence count for Christ every day."

I couldn't get what he had said out of my mind. The following Sunday, I was sitting in church with my wife, Carolyn, when the invitation hymn was sung after the sermon. Without saying a word to anyone, I walked to the front of the church and met the pastor.

He said, "Did you come to pray for someone, Coach?"

Sin in our lives is the biggest giant we will ever face.

I replied, "No, sir. I came to commit everything to God. I want to sell out to the Lord and follow Him in baptism."

He looked startled. He knew that I had always lived a clean life and had read my Bible a lot. He knew I had been involved in the Baptist Student Union as a young man. I was the superintendent of the Young People's Sunday School Department, and I was in church every time the door opened, along with my wife and sons.

What I hadn't done was turn my entire life *completely* over to the Lord and resolve the sin issue in my life once and for all. That was my night to face the giant of my own nature and my own lapse of faith and to turn to God and ask for His forgiveness. That was my night for a spiritual giant of sinfulness and neglect of the things of the Lord to be slain in my life—not by my own doing, but by the Lord Jesus.

A revival broke out in the church that night, and it lasted fourteen days. The high school where I coached became involved in the revival, and before the two weeks were over, some 458 decisions had been made.

The revival spread all across Birmingham, Alabama. I was invited to give my testimony in another large church in Birmingham, the Central Park Baptist Church. I accepted the opportunity to speak, but I was scared to death at the prospect. Teaching students and coaching football players was one thing. Speaking about my relationship with God before two thousand people was something else.

A giant loomed before me. It was a test. Would I confess Christ openly before the group of people and trust God to give me both the words and the courage? Or would I back down, only to face that giant some other day?

I discovered that when it comes to spiritual matters, you make the decisions by your will, and then God gives you the ability and the courage by His Holy Spirit.

The service began. The place was packed. I thought to myself, *I can't do this!* My mouth got dry. I couldn't swallow. The moment seemed overwhelming to me. A thought danced through my mind: *The next time they pray, I'm slipping out. I can tell them I got sick.* It wouldn't have been far from the absolute truth on that point.

The next thing I knew, we were praying. But instead of my making a move, Pastor Johnnie Bob Riddle sensed my fears, reached over, and took my hand. He said, "Don't be afraid. God will use you. Everything will be all right." And it was.

God spoke through me that evening. Among those who walked the aisle at the invitation were pastors and deacons, parents and students.

The last thirty years have been an adventure with the Lord. Philippians 4:13 has become real in my life: "I can do all things through Christ who strengthens me." If you truly believe that verse, you *can't* have grasshopper mentality.

That doesn't mean that I haven't faced giants, including some giants in my spiritual growth and walk with the Lord. The giants have come. But each time, I look at them with this understanding: "God knows this giant is here in my path. God knows this giant is taunting me and coming against one of His children. God not only knows, but He cares, and He's here with me."

I face the giants in my life with the knowledge that the Giant Slayer, Jesus Christ Himself, is with me. I can't slay a giant on my own, but I can slay any giant that comes my way with the Lord by my side, strengthening me with His presence.

If you don't know Jesus Christ as your Savior and Lord today, I invite you to ask Him into your life to slay the sin giant that is keeping you from having a vibrant and loving relationship with your heavenly Father. Ask Him to forgive you for letting this giant limit your life. Ask Him to free you from the bondage of sin and set you free, and to give you the "want to" to live a life that is in right relationship with God. Ask Him to take away your grasshopper mentality and give you the ability to think and believe like a giant slayer.

God not only knows, but He cares.

I believe that if you ask that of God, He will do it. He did it for me. He'll do it for you.

The Lord desires that you live a victorious life in the destiny that He has designed for you. Don't let any giants stand in your way!

Dr. William Mitchell speaks and conducts seminars for educators, parents, churches, and corporations all across the nation and abroad. He also has available video and audio messages and other informative and inspiring materials. For additional information about Dr. Mitchell's services and materials contact:

Dr. William Mitchell
P.O. Box 20037
Myrtle Beach, SC 29575
(803) 650-7677